Roads *Less Traveled*
IN SOUTH–CENTRAL OREGON

A Guide to Back Roads and Special Places

Steve Arndt (signature)

Steve Arndt

About the Roads Less Traveled Series:

"The series will stitch together the state's history and habitat for anyone who pays as much attention to what they're driving through as where they're going." — **Bill Monroe,** *The Oregonian*

www.roadslesstraveledoregon.com

Also by Steve Arndt:

Roads Less Traveled in Northeast Oregon
Roads Less Traveled in North-Central Oregon
Roads Less Traveled in Northwest Oregon I
Roads Less Traveled in Northwest Oregon II
Roads Less Traveled in Southeast Oregon
Roads Less Traveled in Southwest Oregon

Roads Less Traveled in South-Central Oregon
A Guide to Back Roads and Special Places

Steve Arndt

Photographs by
Diane Arndt of Woodburn, Oregon, except
Wagontire Store by Bruce Fingerhood of Springfield, Oregon and
Diane Arndt by Amanda Arndt Vega of Woodburn, Oregon

Maps by
Justin Eslinger, Box Lunch Design

Printed in the United States of America

ISBN: 978-0-9844294-7-9

Front Cover:
    Cultus Lake
    (Photograph by Diane Arndt)

Back Cover (from top to bottom)
    Wooden Grain Storage near Merrill
    Sparks Lake
    Clearwater Falls
    Homestead Open Air Museum in Fort Rock
    Crater Lake and Wizard Island
    (Photographs by Diane Arndt)

Designed by

Justin Eslinger | Box Lunch Design
boxlunchdesign@gmail.com

Dedicated to our parents

Otto P. Arndt
Julia R. Leavitt
Harrison E. Leavitt
Robert M. Gillett
Dorothy A. Sparks
Dale H. Sparks

In memory of our deceased parents, with gratitude
for their love, guidance, and influence in our lives.
Although only one lived to see early editions of *Roads
Less Traveled* in print, we recognize their investments in
us, are grateful for the sacrifices they made for us, and
hope this series of books is a reflection of the positive
and collective values that we inherited.

I shall be telling this with a sigh
Somewhere ages and ages hence:
Two roads diverged in a wood, and I—
I took the one less traveled by,
And that has made all the difference.

—Robert Frost (1874-1963)
from his poem, "The Road Not Taken"

Acknowledgements

Special Thanks to:

Joyce Hardman, Sprague River Librarian,
who loaned me a book

The folks at the Sprague River Community Center,
who stopped their meeting to share information about their town

The good folk of Paisley,
who freely shared about their community

Terry and Sandy Leimbach,
former Woodburn acquaintances that own Pioneer Saloon and Family Restaurant in Paisley

Sally B.,
the proprietor of 'Just Stuff' in New Pine Creek

Folks at Lakeview Chamber of Commerce,
who eagerly and willingly shared information about Lake County

Employees at Lakeview Bank,
who graciously assisted me in providing the history of the bank

The owner/operator of the Westfir Lodge

Oakridge City Hall employees,
for help with names and addresses of old buildings in Oakridge

Bruce Fingerhood of Springfield,
for allowing me use of his photo of Wagontire

An unknown citizen of Fort Klamath,
who gave us a guided tour of the Community Improvement Club building and the freshly painted outhouses

Operators of Klamath Visitors Center,
who went out of their way to help us

The librarian and volunteer at the Chiloquin Visitors Center, and the owners of the local hardware store,
who shared information about the Chiloquin community

The current proprietors of the Olene Store and the neighbors next door (former Olene Store owners),
who graciously assisted us with information

The citizens of Malin,
who stopped to visit with us while we were walking around the old downtown

Bonanza residents,
who helped provide dates and information about their community

The owner of Summer Lake Hot Springs,
who gave us a tour of the facility

All who provided assistance in the production of this book or shared information about their communities, with sincere apologies to anyone not mentioned by name.

Contents

Foreword

It was ten years ago that the idea for the book series, *Roads Less Traveled in Oregon*, was spawned. With one college textbook under my writer's belt, I planned to take a sabbatical leave to write another. The first textbook, *Curriculum Planning and the Role of the Teacher*, was a teacher-directed workbook without a teacher guide, and was used solely in my introductory teaching courses for both elementary and secondary education students. It became a best seller at Warner Pacific College, where I sold anywhere from twenty to sixty copies per year! Students were charged $10 for the guidebook, probably the least expensive text the education students ever purchased.

The workbook for the semester-long course became the curricular backbone text for the teacher education department and included the required lesson plan format that was used in every education course, and that students followed in order to complete all pre-service teaching assignments and work samples. The non-traditionally formatted book was more than 100 pages in length. The second text I planned to write was to be more traditional in structure and approach, including a bibliography and an accompanying CD of classroom situations and scenarios. Several publishers awaited a mock-up of my ideas and a brief synopsis of the proposed book for consideration.

Two weeks before my sabbatical leave, my wife and I took a drive, much as we had for the majority of our married life. We usually left the house with no destination in mind and went places that we had not been. In the late 1970s, we purchased a book by Ralph Friedman titled *Oregon For the Curious*. We made it our goal to take every trip outlined in the book, checking off chapters and places that we visited. Children followed and the trips continued. It became a part of the 'Arndt Culture' to take frequent trips on the back roads of our state. At some point, we found that there were many places in Oregon that were not listed or mentioned in Friedman's book. Thus, we began using it as a springboard to destinations beyond those described. One such trip was the route around the north side of Mt. Hood. For whatever reason, we chose to explore this lesser-known and seldom-used route around Oregon's highest mountain, Mt. Hood, the one Native Americans called *Wy'East*.

We began this trip in Hood River, today known as the Wind Surfing Capital of Oregon. The itinerary wound through the small communities of Odell, Mt. Hood, Parkdale, and Dee. From Dee, we went to Lost Lake, a beautiful setting, 5.7 miles off of the forest road we were taking. After watching eagles fish in the lake and a 'belly timber' stop at the Lost Lake grocery mart, we returned to the forest road and continued around the mountain, past Mt. Hood's most recent (early 1800s) lava flow. We reached the summit of Lolo Pass, which afforded spectacular and panoramic views. We began our descent that included 5.6 miles of well-maintained gravel with a gentle meander hardly slowing our progress around the mountain. Just before reaching the small bergs of Zig Zag and Brightwood, both located near Oregon Highway 26, we took time to walk segments of the Barlow Trail.

It was along this trail that a light bulb literally clicked on in my mind and the book series was spawned. I returned home, never to write a second textbook, but, instead, to write a guide to the back roads of

Foreword

Oregon and its history, wonder, and beauty. I began to research our trip around Mt. Hood and found that most of the Lolo Pass route was actually a Native American trail around the mountain, used for thousands of years during seasonal migration.

The next six months were spent researching, writing, and traveling the northwest and southwest parts of our state. *Roads Less Traveled in Northwest Oregon* and *Roads Less Traveled in Southwest Oregon* slowly came together and were published and released in 2004.

Our curiosity-driven desire to see more of the state was intensified and *Roads Less Traveled in North-Central Oregon* was released, followed by *Roads Less Traveled in Northwest Oregon II*. In our haste to publish, minor printing errors were made, such as 'if for it' and 'of for off.' There were also an unfortunate handful of critical errors, such as telling travelers to turn left when we meant for them to turn right. Second editions were printed, correcting the mistakes, and improving the quality of the books. In late 2007, we submitted the proof copy of *Roads Less Traveled in Northeast Oregon* to be published. For whatever reason, the publisher 'sat on' this book for more than a year, prompting us to end the once-solid relationship that we had formed. Because we were denied use of the book print formats, we were left with only our photos and original, unedited texts. To remain published, we knew we would have to start anew. Thankfully, we learned that this dark cloud indeed had a silver lining.

We started over in 2008, traveling, researching, and expanding every route, and taking more photos with a new camera. Fate led us to Justin Eslinger — a young, talented family friend — who is a professional graphic designer and founder of Box Lunch Design. We submitted our work to Justin who, in my opinion, took the book series from good to great. He expanded the format from two-columns to three, included more and better maps, shade coded points of interest and points en route, and used various tones on the covers to identify similar geographic sectors of the state.

With Justin's help, creative formatting, and advanced design skills, we were able to produce *Roads Less Traveled in Northwest Oregon II* in 2008 - the first book that we self-published. In 2010, we released *Roads Less Traveled in Northeast Oregon*, and re-released *Roads Less Traveled in North-Central Oregon, 2nd edition*. In 2011, we released the 2nd edition of *Roads Less Traveled in NW Oregon I*, and, in 2012 — a busy year for us — we released *Roads Less Traveled in North-Central Oregon, 3rd edition*, *Roads Less Traveled in Southeast Oregon*, and *Roads Less Traveled in Southwest Oregon, 2nd edition*.

This book, *Roads Less Traveled in South-Central Oregon* — the seventh in the series — is scheduled for release in spring of 2013. It brings to an end my ten-year dream and goal of covering the entire state of Oregon! Future tentative plans include compiling a 'Best of the Roads Less Traveled in Oregon' book. On the 'far-back burner' are thoughts about writing another series covering Roads Less Traveled in Southwest and South-Central Washington. Time will dictate our course.

In the meantime, always take the roads less traveled.

Steve Arndt

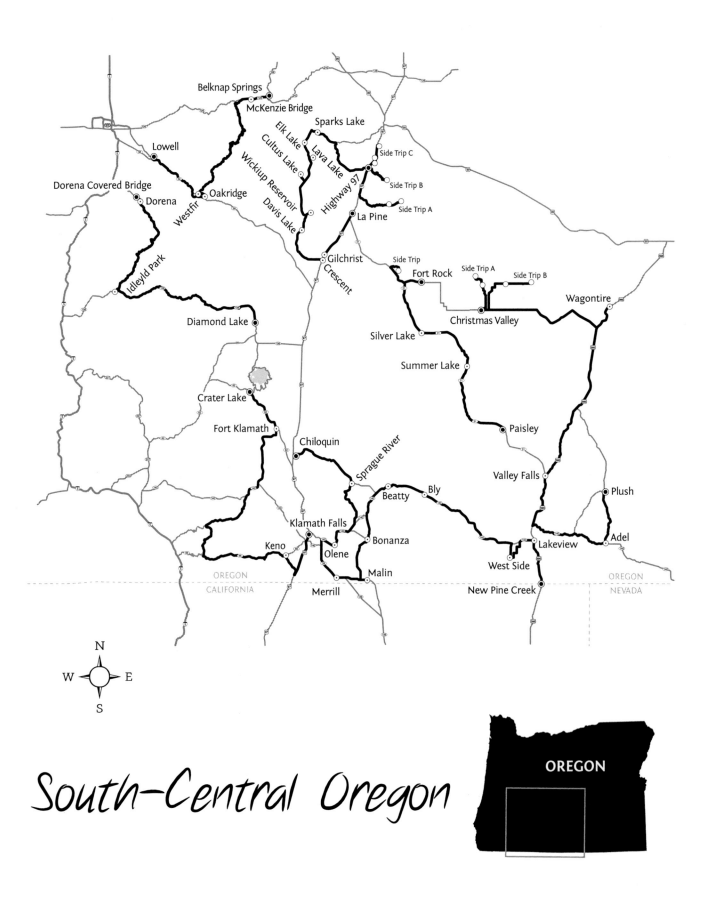

South-Central Oregon

OREGON

Introduction

You might say that this book has been ten years in the making. In 2003, I conceived the *Roads Less Traveled in Oregon* book series with a plan to divide the state into six sections and write a book about each one. This book describes points of interest and history of the places found along routes through the south central section of Oregon, and completes the series. Routes for each of the seven books now in print (two books were written about northwest Oregon) were developed over time and after much thought and research — ten years for this book. The completion of *Roads Less Traveled in South-Central Oregon* fulfills our goal to explore and write about the entire state.

The state of Oregon covers an area that is more than 92,000 square miles. The south central section extends east from Interstate 5 to the Harney County border. From north to south, it includes the area from just south of Bend in Central Oregon to the California border. A majority of routes described in the book are in Lake and Klamath counties, and others take travelers through parts of Douglas and Deschutes counties. In area, Lake County is the third largest in the state, covering 8358 square miles; followed by Klamath County at 5945 square miles. Lake County, named for its large number of lakes and hot springs, was formed in 1874. Klamath County was formed in 1882, twenty-three years after Oregon became a state.

Introduction

The seven routes each comprise a book chapter and are in placed in an order such that travelers can drive them one after the other. Route 1 begins at Belknap Hot Springs, located on Highway 126, about seventy miles east of Eugene. The route ends in the former

mill town of Lowell, adjacent to the Willamette River and Dexter Reservoir. Route 2 begins about thirty miles from Lowell at the Dorena Covered Bridge. This route goes south and then east, ending at Diamond Lake, one of Oregon's finest fishing spots. From Diamond Lake, go south about twenty miles to Crater Lake, and begin route 3. This route ends in Klamath Falls, formerly called Linkville. Route 4 begins in Chiloquin, twenty-six miles north of Klamath Falls. This route takes the traveler east and south, ending in New Pine Creek, a city that was formed on the Oregon and California border. From New Pine, travel north and then east to Plush, where Route 5 begins. Visit the Antelope Refuge before heading south to Adel and then drive toward Lake Abert and Christmas Valley, north of Lakeview. Enjoy side trips to Crack in the Ground, Sand Dunes, and Lost Forest. Dip south to Paisley and start Route 6, which concludes at Fort Rock, with a side trip to Hole in the Ground. From Fort Rock, head north and west to Lapine to begin route 7. From Lapine, travel to Gilchrist, one of the last company towns in Oregon. Continue to the high lakes on Century Drive, then on to Highway 97 at Sunriver. From here, take any or all of three optional routes to Paulina and East Lakes, Lava Cast Forest, and, finally, Lava Lands and High Desert Museum.

Introduction

Before your adventure through South-Central Oregon, test your knowledge of the area by taking the following quiz (answers can be found at the bottom of page 103 and all are explained in the book, *Roads Less Traveled in South-Central Oregon*):

1 What is the Oregon State Gemstone found near Plush?

2 What natural phenomenon occurs in Glide and no other place in the US?

3 The only Americans killed on American soil during WWII died near what city in South-Central Oregon?

4 Near what small town east of Klamath Falls are investors spending millions of dollars tapping and harnessing geothermal energy?

5 What is the name of the geologic fissure, located near Christmas Valley, where the ground has separated from two to six feet for almost two miles?

6 Fort Klamath was the longest-lived fort in Oregon. What Native American Indian Chief was hung at this fort for killing General Canby, for whom Canby, Oregon is named?

7 Due to its lawlessness and rowdy populace, what small town in Klamath County was nicknamed 'Little Chicago'?

8 What is the name of the mine that has produced more gold than any other in the history of the state?

9 Besides being a company town, what was unique about the lumber community of Gilchrist?

10 On Christmas Eve in 1894, what tragic event occurred in the small town of Silver Lake?

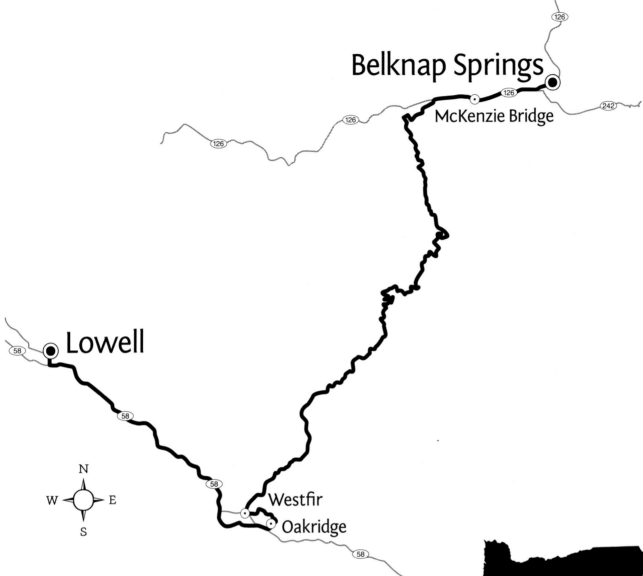

Belknap Springs

McKenzie Bridge

Lowell

Westfir
Oakridge

N
W E
S

OREGON

Belknap Springs
to Lowell

Hot Water and Covered Bridges

Belknap Springs to Lowell (95 miles)

This ninety-five mile trip begins at Belknap Springs and ends in Lowell near a covered bridge with others found along the way, including the longest covered bridge in Oregon. In addition to Belknap, explorers can enjoy hot springs at Cougar and Terwilliger – all located along this mountainous route that includes an important 1860s stagecoach road. While at McKenzie Bridge, imagine loaded wagons navigating the McKenzie River as they carried necessary supplies east and west across the Cascades in the late 1800s.

Farther on, explore a section of Aufderheide Memorial Drive – one of the most picturesque routes in Oregon, and more than 140 miles if driven in totality. Views from several locations in the Willamette National Forest are nothing short of spectacular, so pack a lunch or snack to enjoy while stopping at any of the scenic pullouts along the way.

An alert traveler might spot a cougar or other wild animal that lives in abundance along a sixty-mile stretch of paved road with occasional washouts that are frequently repaired. Before you head out, be sure to check road and weather condition reports because snow frequently blocks this route October through May.

Rail yard in Oakridge

Belknap Springs

Elevation: 1611 feet

Location:
44.11.553 N • 122.09.052 W

Services:
food, lodging, camping, RV

Belknap Hot Springs and Resort

Explorers George Millican, John T. Craig, James Storment, and Joseph Carter discovered the hot springs in 1854. In November, 1869, Rollin. S. Belknap conceived his idea to build a health resort and mineral spa at this location. A post office opened here in 1874 as Salt Springs. The name was changed to Belknaps Springs in 1875 and amended to Belknap Springs in 1891. The office closed in 1953, after merging with the McKenzie Bridge postal service. The hot springs' water emerges from the ground at sixty gallons a minute, averaging between 185 and 195 degrees, and must be cooled before it goes into the pool. The mineral spa has been a destination sought by bathers for more than 100 years. Evidence of Native American habitation in the area dates to over 8000 years. Warm Springs Tribes migrated through the area as late as the early 1900s.

Point of Interest

- **Belknap Hot Springs and Resort**
  (59296 Belknap Springs Road)
  Established in 1874, the resort has two mineral pools, seven cabins, fifteen tent sites, eighteen lodge rooms, and forty-two RV sites.

Belknap Springs to McKenzie Bridge

Distance:
5.9 miles

Directions:
From Belknap Hot Springs Lodge, go west toward Highway 126.

Points En Route

(mileage from Belknap Hot Springs and Resort)

0.3 miles:
Turn right onto Highway 126.

0.7 miles:
Crossing Lost Creek.

2.1 miles:
Paradise Campground.

3.5 miles:
McKenzie River Ranger Station (1934). Scenic Byway Information Center and location of the old CCC Camp Belknap.

5.0 miles:
Leaving Willamette National Forest.

5.5 miles:
Jennie B. Harris Wayside. Picnicking and fishing.

5.9 miles:
McKenzie Bridge

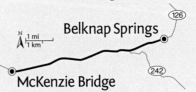

McKenzie Bridge

Elevation: 1362 feet

Location:
44.10.471 N • 122.09.346 W

Services:
food, camping, RV

On the stagecoach road from Eugene to Central Oregon, McKenzie Bridge was an important stagecoach river crossing. First called McInzie Bridge, the name changed to McKenzie Bridge in 1918. John Templeton Craig, who is buried here, lived near the river in the 1860s and was an ardent supporter of road development across the Cascade Range. The area was first known as Strawberry Prairie because many wild strawberries grew in the grassy meadow near the river. In 2006, a horrendous fire destroyed most of the 1890s Log Cabin Inn, which is listed on the National Historic Registry.

Hayes Homestead

Points of Interest

- **General Store**
  (91837 Taylor Creek Road)
  In the 1950s, gas pumps stood at the entrance of the store.

- **Hayes Homestead**
  (located behind the general store at 91821 Taylor Creek Road)
  Built in 1920.

- **Log Cabin Inn**
  (across the street from the store)
  Even though most of the 1890s Inn was destroyed by fire, one of the old buildings remains. Herbert Hoover, Clark Gable, and the Duke of Windsor stayed at the historic inn.

- **McKenzie Covered Bridge**
  The first bridge was constructed in 1911 and replaced in 1939. The 1939 bridge was destroyed during the Christmas Flood of 1964 and rebuilt in 1966.

Cascade Park

McKenzie Bridge to Westfir

Distance:
62.9 miles

Directions:
From the McKenzie General Store, proceed west on Highway 126.

Points En Route

(mileage from the general store)

Note: No gas for 70 miles. The road is frequently closed from October to May.

0.5 miles:
McKenzie Bridge Campground.

1.2 miles:
Turn left onto McKenzie River Loop and travel toward Rainbow.

1.4 miles:
Patio RV Park.

3.3 miles:
Upper McKenzie Community Center.

3.4 miles:
Former settlement of Rainbow. Mrs. L. Quimby named the unincorporated community for the abundance of rainbow trout in the river, after her husband bought the property and established a post office at this location in 1924. The office closed in 1937. Turn left onto W. King Road and cross the Belknap Covered Bridge.

3.5 miles:
Stop sign. Turn right to follow W. King Road (paved but lacks striping).

5.1 miles:
Stop sign. Turn right onto Cougar Dam Road (two-lanes and striped).

5.5 miles:
Turn left onto Aufderheide Drive and travel toward Cougar Reservoir. This road was named to honor Robert Aufderheide, a Willamette National Forest supervisor who died in 1959.

8.7 miles:
Cougar Dam and Reservoir.

12.5 miles:
Gravel road for 0.1 miles.

12.6 miles:
Pavement returns.

12.8 miles:
Terwilliger Hot Springs.

14.9 miles:
Crossing the South Fork of the McKenzie River.

15.0 miles:
Cougar Crossing Campground and information kiosk. The winding road narrows. There are occasional pullouts for river access.

16.4 miles:
French Pete Campground.

16.9 miles:
Stay straight.

19.5 miles:
Rebel Trailhead.

20.3 miles:
Red Diamond Campground.

Belknap Covered Bridge

Cougar Dam and Reservoir

McKenzie Bridge

126

N 5 mi
   5 km

Westfir

Westfir

Elevation: 1075 feet

Location:
43.45.497 N • 122.29.703 W

Services:
groceries, B&B

The name Westfir was first used in 1923 and described the business activities of the Western Lumber Company. The WLC quickly formed a company town and in 1923 a post office opened. In 1946, Edward Hines, of Central Oregon lumber fame, took over mill operations and the company-owned community. Hines opened a plywood division here in 1952 and successfully ran the mill and town until 1977, when the mill closed and the company sold all of its holdings, including the homes, mill buildings and equipment, and the water and sewer infrastructure. By 1979, Westfir was independent and incorporated shortly thereafter. A 1984 fire destroyed the mill and ended all lumber manufacturing.

Office Covered Bridge

Points of Interest

- **Office Covered Bridge**
  (on Westfir-Oakridge Road off North Fork Road)
  The longest covered bridge in Oregon, built in 1944, was used to connect the lumber office with the mill. Cross the bridge to the old mill site and current location of a city park.

- **Westfir Lodge** *(47365 1st)*
  Formerly the 6270 square-foot home of the Westfir Lumber Company, the 1952 building was converted into a Bed and Breakfast in 1991.

Westfir to Oakridge

Distance:
3.3 miles

Directions:
From the Post Office and General Store, drive east on West Oak Road.

Points En Route

(mileage from the General Store)

0.1 miles:
Westfir City Hall.

1.7 miles:
Keep right.

2.4 miles:
Circle Bar Golf Course.

2.9 miles:
Stay right.

3.3 miles:
Oakridge

Elevation: 1244 feet

Location:
43.44.850 N • 122.22.893 W

Services:
gas, food, lodging, RV

In 1852, members of a scouting party, who were searching for routes from the Willamette Valley over the Cascades to Central Oregon, were the first to explore the Oakridge area, calling it Big Prairie. In the 1860s, the Sanford Brothers built a ranch in what is now Oakridge. For more than fifty years very little development occurred until 1910 when the railroad was established. First known as Hazeldell and later Oakridge, the small town blossomed into a timber community. The Oakridge Post Office opened in 1912 and the town incorporated in 1934. Shortly after WWII, Pope and Talbot opened a lumber mill that employed over 500 workers. The community grew and, at its peak, more than 5000 people called Oakridge home, in sharp contrast to the declining population today. The Pope and Talbot wood products boom ended in 1986 when the mill closed, creating an economic crisis for the small town. The city now owns the property where the mill that kept the community afloat for over forty years once stood. Oakridge is known as the Mountain Biking Capital of the Northwest. The annual Oakridge Tree Planting Festival started in 1953.

IOOF Hall

Points of Interest

- **IOOF Hall** (*1st and Hazel*)
  Built in 1922 as a dance hall, the second story, used by the Odd Fellows, was added in 1925.

- **Paddocks Hardware**
  (*1st between Pine and Hazel*)
  Constructed in 1925. The upstairs houses six apartments.

- **Smith's Store** (*1st and Pine*)
  Established in the early 1930s.

- **US Forest Service Building and Post Office** (*48246 1st*)
  1912.

- **Oakridge City Hall** (*1st and Ash*)
  1953. A historical marker in front of the building tells of the Free Emigrant Road that more than 2000 pioneers followed in the 1850s.

- **Oakridge Livery Stable** (*48334 1st*)
  In 1915, this building served as a livery stable and blacksmith shop.

- **Pioneer Museum** (*76433 Pine*)
  Originally the 1920 Oakridge newspaper office, it became the museum in 1959.

- **Oakridge Bank**
  Opened in 1947 and is now the Corner Bar and Grill.

- **St. Michael's Catholic Church** (*76387 Crestview*)
  Early 1910s.

- **Greenspring Park** (*48362 Highway 58*)
  South of town and home to an old log cabin.

- **Kitson Hot Springs** (*several miles southeast near Hills Creek Reservoir*)
  A popular place to soak for both locals and travelers.

St. Michael's Catholic Church

Oakridge to Lowell

Distance:
22.7 miles

Directions:
From the intersection of Highway 58 and Crestview Street, drive west on Highway 58.

Points En Route

(mileage from the stop light at the intersection)

0.2 miles:
Old water tower.

4.0 miles:
Middle Fork Ranger Station.

5.5 miles:
Elevation: 1000 feet. The Willamette River parallels the highway.

8.2 miles:
Black Canyon Campground.

9.6 miles:
Hampton Campground and boat launch.

11.3 miles:
Hiking trail to the left and Lookout Reservoir to the right.

14.6 miles:
Rest area with pit toilet.

16.1 miles:
Leaving Willamette National Forest.

20.8 miles:
Viewpoint.

22.2 miles:
Turn right onto Jasper-Lowell Road.

22.4 miles:
The 1945 Lowell Covered Bridge and rest area with an excellent view of the dam and mountains. When the dam was completed in 1954, the reservoir buried the communities of Carter, Landax and Reserve. In 1846, Elijah Bristow settled in the area. In 1853, Elijah Elliot helped rescue members of the lost wagon train near this point.

22.7 miles:
Lowell

Lowell Covered Bridge

Lowell

Elevation: 725 feet

Location:
43.55.118 N • 122.47.051 W

Services:
gas, food

Amos Hyland, who came from Lowell, Maine in the late 1850s, named the community. Hyland, who helped secure the post office, served as its postmaster. Hyland also operated a successful livestock ranch and had fourteen children, all born and raised on his ranch. The original 1890 post office was named Cannon and then changed to Lowell in 1893. The railroad came to Lowell in 1908, and it soon became an important trading center. The city incorporated in 1954. When lumber mills ran 'round the clock, Lowell boasted of a roller skating rink, pool hall, liquor store, hotel, dentist, shoe store, two barbershops, three cafés, and five gas stations. Ten million years ago, Redwood trees grew abundantly in the area. A catastrophic landslide uncovered petrified trees on the south side of Disappointment Butte (north of town).

Lowell High School

Points of Interest

- **Lowell Grange** (*51 2nd*)
  Originally the 1913 school, the building was purchased by the grange in 1930.

- **Lowell High School**
  (*65 S Pioneer*)
  Built in 1930 to replace the old school that is now the grange. The elementary school, built in the early 1940s, is located adjacent to the high school.

- **City Hall** (*107 3rd*)
  Adjacent to the civic center is Rolling Rock City Park. Amenities include a picnic area, 1988 covered walking bridge, logging memorabilia, and restrooms. Look for a large piece of petrified wood that was found locally.

- **Hyland Cemetery**
  (*245 N Hyland*)
  Formerly called Howe Cemetery, the first burial took place in 1875.

Lowell Grange

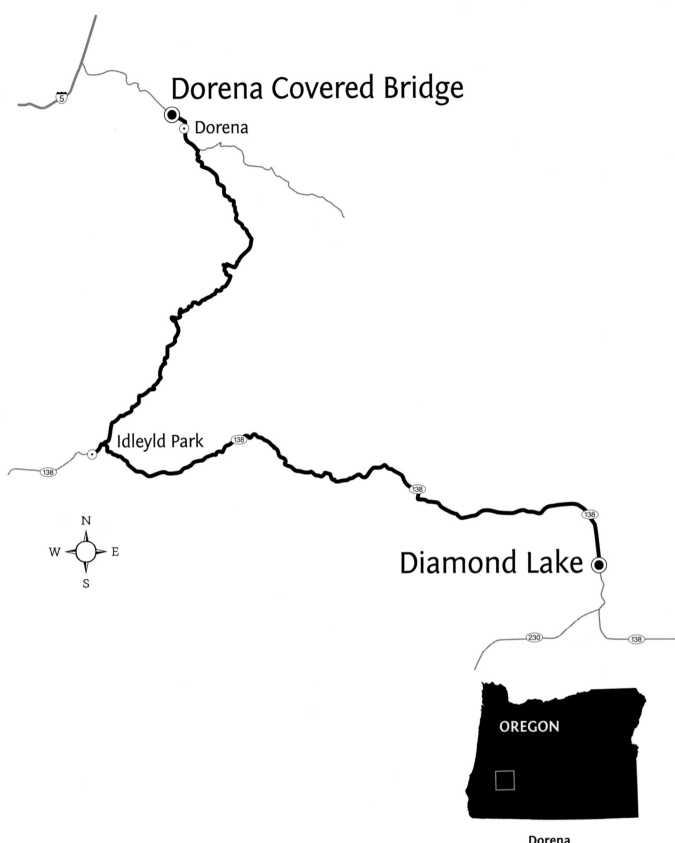

Dorena Covered Bridge

Dorena to Diamond Lake

Oregon's Largest Mine, Colliding Rivers, and Waterfalls

Dorena to Diamond Lake (111 miles)

From the Dorena Covered Bridge, roughly eight miles east of Cottage Grove, this route meanders through hills that lead to more than forty miles through sections of Willamette and Umpqua National Forests where Douglas Fir and a variety of softwood trees tower in the landscape. Mid-trip, explorers can venture to the Bohemian Mine, Oregon's longest running gold mine. Be alert for bears, cougars, wildcats, and other animals that are frequently spotted in the area.

The route includes a stop in Glide to witness the North Umpqua River and the Little River dramatically and powerfully collide. Waterfalls aplenty follow – some of which can be easily viewed and others require a longer hike. The self-guided tour ends at Diamond Lake, one of Oregon's most famous fishing destinations, where bold chipmunks dare to steal food from the plates of patio diners.

Whitehorse Falls

Dorena Covered Bridge

Elevation: 975 feet

Location:
43.44.268 N • 122.52.804 W

Services:
none

This 1949 covered bridge, that spans the Row River (rhymes with now), was built near the time the Dorena Dam was constructed. The bridge was once known as the 'Star Bridge' because it afforded access to the Star Ranch, a once grand estate that has been reduced to about 100 acres. In order to preserve it, the state bypassed the covered bridge by building an adjacent concrete bridge in 1974. The Star Bridge was eventually renamed Dorena - the same as the community that was named for *Dora* Burnette and *Rena* Martin. The original Dorena town site lies at the bottom of the reservoir under water. More than 100 homes were moved and some of the buildings, including the 1896 schoolhouse and 1899 post office, were razed in order to make way for the reservoir. The bridge is more than 100-feet long and is designed with Howe Trusses, daylight roofline windows, and a shingle roof.

Dorena Covered Bridge

Dorena Covered Bridge to Dorena

Distance:
1.8 miles

Directions:
From Dorena Covered Bridge, travel east on Row River Highway.

Points En Route

(mileage from the covered bridge)

0.2 miles:
Dorena School.

1.8 miles:
Dorena

Dorena Covered Bridge

N   2000 ft
    500 m

Dorena

Dorena

Elevation: 944 feet

Location:
43.45.16.157 N • 122.51.795 W

Services:
gas, food

The newer town of Dorena was relocated to this spot along the Row River. Much of the community, including the newer post office, can be found on the other side of the bridge, located near the store. The names of two women, Dora Burnette and Rena Martin, were combined to give the community its moniker. The first settlers arrived in the area in the 1850s and farmed the land. Gold that settlers discovered in the creek and in the nearby mountain was quickly removed.

Points of Interest

- **Dorena Mercantile**
  (35750 Row River Road)
  Built in 1950, the store was remodeled and reopened in 2004.

- **Dorena Post Office**
  (located across the bridge)
  The original post office opened in 1899.

Dorena Mercantile

Dorena School

Dorena to Idleyld Park

Distance:
> 42.6 miles

Directions:
> From the Dorena Store, drive east on the Row River Highway.

Points En Route

(mileage from the Dorena Mercantile)

Note: No services for the next 43 miles.

0.8 miles:
> Former Culp Creek Store and gas station, now Boyd's Trailer Park. Culp Creek is an unincorporated community along the Row River. John Culp, who set up a logging camp near the creek that now bears his name, established the community in about 1900. The Culp Creek Post Office opened in 1925 and closed in 2009. A large mill operated from 1959 until 1990 at this location. More than twenty mills existed along the Row River during the lumber industry hey-day. The 1926 silent film "The General" was filmed here.

1.3 miles:
> Culp Creek Trailhead.

2.2 miles:
> Child's Way Charter School. Turn right onto Sharp's Creek Road.

5.0 miles:
> Pines mixed with firs dot the landscape. The road follows Sharp's Creek for the next 8.4 miles.

5.3 miles:
> Sharp's Creek Recreation Area.

11.7 miles:
> Entering Umpqua National Forest. The road narrows.

12.3 miles:
> Turn right onto Clark Creek Road. This is a one-lane, paved road with many turnouts. Note that the gravel road to the left leads to the Bohemian Mine, Oregon's largest producer of gold (eight miles and not recommended in winter).

13.0 miles:
> Keep right toward Steamboat and Highway 138.

18.1 miles:
> Keep right on Rock Creek Road.

19.3 miles:
> Elevation, 3901 feet. This is the summit of Huckleberry Mountain Pass. Panoramic view to the west.

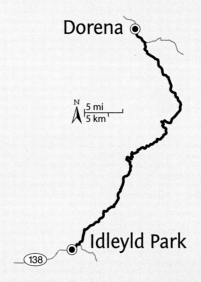

Huckleberry Mountain Pass

Idleyld Park

Elevation: 3971 feet

Location:
43.19.402 N • 123.00.996 W

Services:
gas, food, lodging, RV

Historians are not certain how the name Idleyld Park originated. Early records indicate the area was once called Tioga and changed to Hoaglin. *Tioga* is Iroquois (a Native American tribe in Pennsylvania) for *'where it forks.'* The Tioga Post Office opened in 1890 and was discontinued two years later. *Hoaglin*, also a Native American word, means *'medicine.'* A community named Hoaglin exists in Ohio, where Ohioan emigrants may have inhabited the area in the 1890s. For whatever reason, the post office reopened in 1932 as Idleyld Park. Some think it was named after an amusement park in California. The community is small and relatively new, but offers travelers food and comfort after a beautiful drive through the mountains.

Colliding Rivers

22.8 miles:
Go left onto Rock Creek Road.

33.7 miles:
Stay left.

34.9 miles:
Rock Creek Recreation Site.

36.2 miles:
Rock Creek Maintenance Station.

36.6 miles:
Lone Pine Group Camp.

36.7 miles:
Millpond Recreation Site.

37.9 miles:
The first house in many miles.

40.6 miles:
Two-lane, striped road returns.

41.1 miles:
Rock Creek Fish Hatchery.

41.8 miles:
Stop. Turn right onto Highway 138 and travel toward Roseburg.

42.6 miles:
Idleyld Park

Point of Interest

- **Colliding Rivers** (*drive north 3.4 miles on Highway 238 to Glide*) This is the only place in the United States where two rivers meet head-on. The North Umpqua and Little River collide dramatically at this location. Interpretive exhibits that explain the phenomenon are located in a CCC cabin (open from May until October) adjacent to the parking area.

Idleyld Park to Diamond Lake

Distance:
67.0 miles

Directions:
From the Idleyld Park Store and Deli, at Homestead Avenue and Highway 138, drive east, backtracking on Highway 138.

Points En Route

(mileage form the Idleyld Park Store and Deli)

Note: No gas for 67 miles.

0.1 miles:
The Narrows Wayside. Pit toilet, picnic area. The river narrows to a chute at this point. There is a short hike to the vista point.

0.8 miles:
Continue on Highway 138. This is the intersection with Highway 78 (Rock Creek Road) that leads back to Dorena.

1.0 miles:
Swiftwater Park and Umpqua Trailhead. There is a short hike to Deadline Falls, a short, but massive waterfall.

1.3 miles:
Entering Umpqua artificial fly and lure-only fishing area.

3.4 miles:
Baker Wayside.

7.7 miles:
Susan Creek Recreation Site. A 0.8-mile hike, rated easy, leads to Susan Creek Falls.

11.2 miles:
Fall Creek Falls. Take a moderate, one-mile hike to these falls.

12.6 miles:
North Umpqua Trail Head.

13.4 miles:
Bogus Creek Recreation Site.

15.7 miles:
Crossing Williams Creek.

17.0 miles:
Highway 138 parallels the Umpqua River. Steamboat Inn, food and lodging.

17.5 miles:
Crossing Steamboat Creek. Access a hike to Little Falls, located on Steamboat Creek, by traveling 1.3 miles up Steamboat Road (#38). Steamboat Falls is located 5.3 miles from the highway. Follow Road 38 to Forest Road 3810 and travel 0.6 miles.

17.8 miles:
North Umpqua Trail Access.

18.4 miles:
Gravel Bin raft takeout.

18.6 miles:
Island Campground.

22.1 miles:
Apple Creek and North Umpqua Trail Access.

24.7 miles:
Elevation: 1500 feet.

25.1 miles:
Horseshoe Bend and North Umpqua Trail access.

Toketee Falls

Watson Falls

25.8 miles:
Dry Creek Store.

26.0 miles:
Last Resort Campground and RV.

28.6 miles:
Twin Lakes and North Umpqua Trail access. The Umpqua River now appears on the left.

29.2 miles:
Eagle Rock Campground.

29.7 miles:
Crossing Copeland Creek.

31.0 miles:
Boulder Flat Campground.

33.6 miles:
North Umpqua Trail Access.

35.0 miles:
Elevation: 2000 feet.

37.6 miles:
Toketee Falls and Toketee Lake access road. The hike to the falls is a moderate 0.4 miles climb. More than 200 steps lead to an observation platform. *Toketee* is Chinook jargon for *'pretty'* or *'graceful.'* The falls drop about 80 feet.

39.4 miles:
Toketee Ranger Station.

39.8 miles:
Watson Falls. Day-use only. The short, moderate hike to these falls is 0.4 miles. Watson Falls, the highest in southwest Oregon, plunges more than 270 feet over a ledge of basalt.

40.4 miles:
Elevation: 3000 feet.

43.3 miles:
Elevation: 3500 feet.

44.5 miles:
Whitehorse Falls Campground. An easy, short hike to the fifteen-foot falls.

45.6 miles:
Stump Lake.

48.1 miles:
Clearwater Falls. Camping, picnicking, restrooms. The hike to view the thirty-foot falls is less than 500 feet.

51.2 miles:
Lemolo Lake Recreation Area. Resort access.

54.5 miles:
Elevation: 5000 feet.

57.1 miles:
Diamond Lake Recreation Area. Turn right onto Diamond Lake Loop Road.

67.0 miles:
Diamond Lake

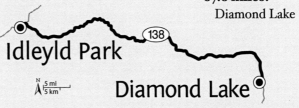

Clearwater Falls

Diamond Lake

Elevation: 5182 feet

Location:
43.10.684 N • 122.03.155 W

Services:
gas, food, lodging, RV

Diamond Lake, located almost one mile above sea level, is one of Oregon's premier fishing and recreation locations. Five boat ramps exist around the lake – all with paved access. The lake was named after John Diamond, an early Coburg, Oregon settler, who discovered the lake in 1852. Diamond Peak is also named after him. The resort, located at the east end of the lake, was constructed in the early 1920s and has expanded to meet growing needs of sportsmen. It is open year-round

Diamond Lake Lodge

and is best known for its abundance of rainbow trout. More than 300 miles of snowmobile trails exist in the Diamond Lake area. In addition to fishing and snowmobiling, popular activities include boating, biking, hiking, horseback riding, snow shoeing, skiing, sled dog racing, inner tubing, hunting, wildlife viewing, and bird watching. In 1938, CCC workers constructed the visitor center that is open from Memorial Day through Labor Day. The lake is nestled between Mt. Thielsen (to the east) and Mt. Bailey (to the west), and affords excellent views of both mountains. Trails connect the lake to the summits of both mountains. The lake is roughly 1.5 miles wide and 3.5 miles long and covers more than 3000 acres. At its greatest depth, the lake is about fifty-two feet. The Diamond Lake Post Office operated from 1925 until 1956. In 2007, it reopened with a summer-only schedule. In 2006, rotenone was used to kill more than 95 million Tui Chub, an invasive species that changed the ecosystem of the lake. Unfortunately, fishermen have used Golden Shiner as bait, introducing another invasive species, and causing Oregon Fish and Wildlife Department much concern.

Points of Interest

- **Diamond Lake Resort**
  (Diamond Lake Loop, east end of the lake)
  The original lodge was built in the 1920s and the visitor's center in 1938. The now modern, full-service, year-round resort offers a boat launch, motel, marina, boat rentals, horse rentals, restaurants, stores, cabins, camping, RV hookups, and other services.

- **Diamond Lake RV Park**
  (3500 Diamond Lake Loop)
  Open May 15th to October 1st.

- **Diamond Lake Corrals**
  (750 Diamond Lake Corrals)
  Operated by the Watson family since 1969. The headquarters are reminiscent of an old western town.

- **Diamond Lake Campground**
  (east side of the lake)
  240 campsites.

- **Broken Arrow Campground**
  (south end of the lake)
  148 campsites.

- **South Shore Area**
  (south shore of the lake)
  Five campsites, playground, volleyball court, horseshoe pits, swimming beach, and picnic accommodations.

- **Thielsen View Campground**
  (west shore of the lake)
  Fifty-eight campsites.

Diamond Lake

Bold chipmunk at lunch

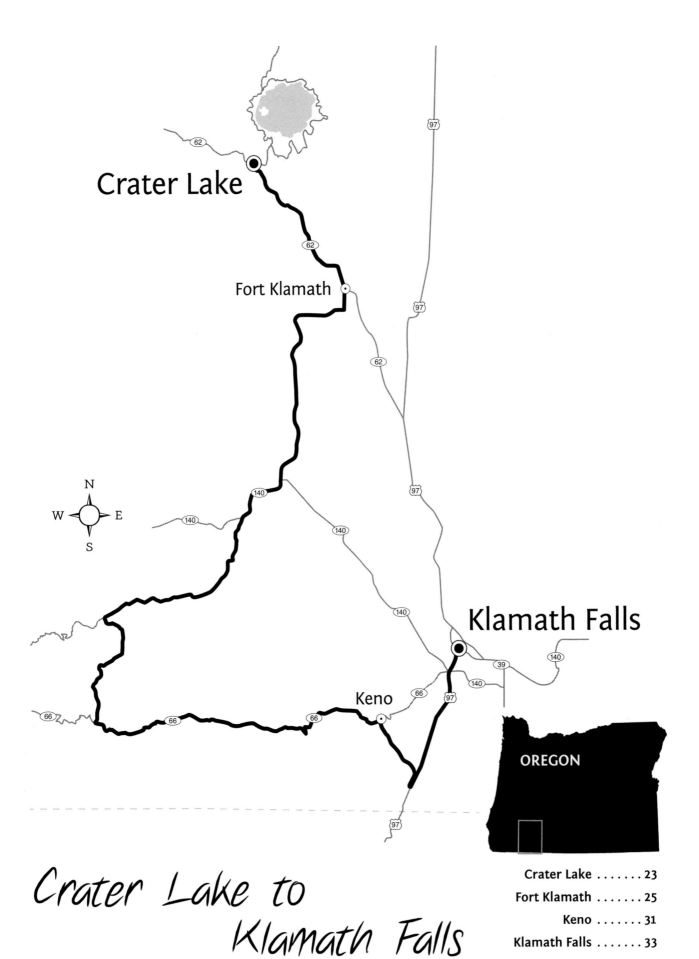

Crater Lake to Klamath Falls

From the Deepest Lake in the US to Pelicans in the Sky

Crater Lake to Klamath Falls (131 miles)

This route begins at Crater Lake, Oregon's only National Park. First seen by white men in 1853, the lake is the cleanest and deepest in the United States. A trip to Crater Lake should be on every Oregonian's bucket list. From the lake, travel to Fort Klamath, a historic community where Captain Jack and three of his warriors were hanged for the murder of General Edward Canby.

Three-fourths of this tour takes place from Fort Klamath to Keno, a stretch of more than ninety miles. Several small communities, an old wagon road and stage stop, and the Applegate Trail, exist on this route. Numerous hiking trails, waterfalls, reservoirs, and lakes await the explorer.

After crossing the Cascades, the journey ends in Klamath Falls where numerous homes and businesses are more than one hundred years old and flocks of pelican (the Klamath Falls High School mascot) fly gracefully overhead. Poet Ogden Nash wrote, *"A wonderful bird is the pelican, / Its bill can hold more than its belly can."*

Wizard Island and Crater Lake

Crater Lake

Elevation: 7305 feet

Location:
42.57.919 N • 122.09.065 W

Services:
gas, food, lodging, RV

It took more than 400,000 years and numerous eruptions to form Mt. Mazama, a once-tall mountain over 12,000 feet. Mt. Mazama blew its top for the final time about 7700 years ago when a huge column of ash and pumice was thrown upward from a vent in the northeast portion of the summit. Prior to the violent eruption, Mt. Mazama's base diameter was more than six miles. New vents formed and the mountain collapsed, forming a deep caldera.

Crater Lake Lodge

Slowly the basin filled with rain and snowmelt (no creeks or streams run into the lake). Wizard Island, a second volcano, erupted after the lake began to form. The lake, known to Native Americans for centuries, was first seen by emigrants in 1853. While searching for gold, prospector John Hillman climbed to the edge of the crater. Through the work of William Gladstone Steel and others, Crater Lake became a National Park. Crater Lake, the deepest and clearest lake in the United States, is located approximately twenty miles off of Highway 97, and has a depth of almost 2000 feet, making it the seventh deepest in the world. The area receives more than 500 inches of snow each year. Rooms are available at the historic lodge but reservations are highly recommended.

Points of Interest

- **Rim Drive**
  A thirty-three mile-long drive circles the lake. The route has more than thirty pullouts, many with interpretive exhibits.

- **Discovery Point**
  Where prospector John Hillman first saw the lake in 1853 while searching for gold.

- **Wizard Island**
  A cinder cone, this 'volcano within a volcano' erupted about 7300 years ago.

- **Pumice Castle Overlook**
  Erosion has carved layers of brightly colored orange pumice stone into the shape of a castle.

- **Phantom Ship**
  Formed by lava more than 400,000 years ago, it is the oldest exposed rock in the caldera.

- **Pinnacles**
  Colored spires tower more than 100 feet above the canyon floor. The pinnacles are actually fossil fumaroles formed when volcanic gasses came through layers of ash, cementing the ash into rock.

- **Vidae Falls**
  A spring-fed creek cascades over a glacier-carved cliff and drops about 100 feet.

- **Crater Lake Lodge**
  The seventy-one room lodge opened in 1915.

- **Crater Lake Boat Tour**
  Purchase tickets in advance and then take the strenuous Cleetwood Cove Trail hike to reach the boat launch.

Crater Lake

Crater Lake to Fort Klamath

Distance:
15.6 miles

Directions:
From the south park entrance kiosk near Mazama Village, drive on Highway 62 toward Klamath Falls.

Points En Route

(mileage from the south park entrance)

0.2 miles:
Turn left onto Highway 62. Travel toward Klamath Falls.

2.6 miles:
Lodgepole Picnic Area access.

4.8 miles:
Annie Falls. Scattered pullouts and canyon viewpoints exist for the next mile.

9.1 miles:
Ponderosa Picnic area. Restrooms.

9.8 miles:
Entering Winema National Forest.

11.0 miles:
The floor of the Klamath Basin.

13.4 miles:
Viewpoint.

15.6 miles:
Fort Klamath

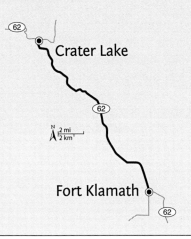

Fort Klamath

Elevation: 4334 feet

Location:
42.42.194 N • 121.59.754 W

Services:
food, lodging, RV, B&B

Fort Klamath was established in 1863. Klamath, from the Klamath Indian word *Iukak*, means *'in the midst'* or *'between two mountains.'* Two companies of soldiers occupied the fort that stood about one mile from the present community from 1863 until 1889. More than fifty buildings, including a sawmill, comprised the fort. Four Modoc warriors, including Chief Kintpuash (Captain Jack), were executed at the fort and are buried on the grounds. The warriors were put to death for their involvement in killing General Edward Canby, for whom the Willamette Valley community is named. Open to visitors, the fort museum is designed after the original guardhouse and is situated at its exact location. The post office opened in 1879 and closed in 1889. The community was platted in 1902 but has never incorporated.

Fort Klamath Civic Improvement Club

Points of Interest

- **Fort Klamath Store**
  (52620 Highway 62)
  The store, built in 1922, closed many years ago.

- **Fort Klamath Civic Improvement Club**
  (near the store)
  The original section of the CIC clubhouse was constructed in 1924 and two additions were built since. A recently painted and decorated 'two-seater outhouse' sits behind the main building.

- **Methodist Church**
  (across the road from the CIC on 2nd Street)
  1912.

Methodist Church

- **Fort Klamath Schoolhouse**
  (0.2 miles west on Nicholson Road)
  The old red schoolhouse was built in 1902.

- **Nicholson Ranch**
  (0.8 miles west on Nicholson Road)
  The road is named for these early farmers.

- **Nicholson Dairy Farm**
  (1.6 miles west on Nicholson Road)
  One of the many dairies that once blanketed the area around Fort Klamath.

- **Fort Klamath Cemetery**
  (1.0 miles east on Highway 62)
  This cemetery dates to the 1870s and is the 1873 burial site of Chief Kintpuash, better known as Captain Jack.

- **Site of Fort Klamath Historical Marker** *(1.4 miles east of town on Highway 62)*
  Fort Klamath was the longest-lived fort in Oregon, operating for twenty-six years.

- **Fort Klamath County Park and Military Post/Museum**
  (1.6 miles east of town on Highway 62 at 51400 Klamath Highway)
  The military post was established in 1863 and closed in 1889.

Fort Klamath Schoolhouse

Fort Klamath Hotel

Fort Klamath to Keno

Distance:
93.9 miles

Directions:
From the CIC building, drive south on Highway 62. In 0.2 miles, Highway 62 curves to the left. Do not go left; go straight across onto Weed Road, heading south toward Klamath Falls. Gas up before you go.

Points En Route

(mileage from the CIC building)

0.2 miles:
Drive straight ahead onto Weed Road (not marked) and proceed south. Do not curve left on Highway 62.

1.9 miles:
Turn right onto Sevenmile Road.

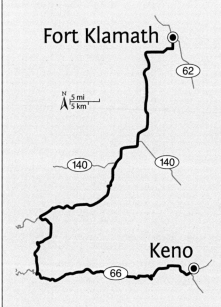

6.9 miles:
Entering Winema National Forest.

11.2 miles:
Nannie Creek Trailhead.

12.4 miles:
Cherry Creek Trailhead.

17.1 miles:
Malone Springs.

20.3 miles:
Rocky Point Resort and site of Rocky Point. Rocky Point, a descriptive name, is located on Pelican Bay. The post office, originally called Pelican, opened in 1888. Two more name changes occurred – the first in 1907 to Ashland and the second in 1915 to Recreation – before the post office was called Rocky Point. This name was used from 1924 until 1947 when the name was changed once again – this time to Harriman. The Harriman Post Office closed for good in 1954. A rail station existed here at one time, but the railroad no longer serves the small community. In 1903, President Teddy Roosevelt stayed in Rocky Point at the Pelican Bay Resort. The Resort burned to the ground in 1942. The Point Comfort Lodge (also known as The White Pelican) was a notorious brothel. Sturgeon, planted in 1956, are said to be in excess of 400 pounds and can often be seen near the surface of Klamath Lake at this location.

23.4 miles:
Turn right onto Highway 140, traveling toward Lake of the Woods and Medford.

23.7 miles:
Varney Creek Road Organizational Camp access.

26.1 miles:
Cold Springs Trailhead access road.

29.3 miles:
Turn left onto Dead Indian Memorial Highway. The area was named in 1854 after settlers found two dead Native Americans in their wigwams near the creek near the lake.

30.8 miles:
Lake of the Woods Resort. Lake of the Woods is a three and a half-mile-wide lake that is fed by snow melt from Mount McLoughlin. A post office opened here in 1930 and abruptly closed in 1931.

31.7 miles:
Sunset Campground and boat launch.

32.9 miles:
Low Echo Organizational Camp.

37.4 miles:
Lake of the Woods Village.

38.1 miles:
Leaving Winema Forest and entering Rogue-Siskiyou National Forest.

38.6 miles:
Pacific Crest Trail access and parking area.

39.4 miles:
Entering Jackson County.

42.9 miles:
Marsh area.

44.0 miles:
Sno-Park (the route continues straight on Dead Indian Memorial Highway).

44.7 miles:
Leaving Rogue-Siskiyou National Forest.

47.2 miles:
Wilderness Trails Youth Camp.

47.5 miles:
Lily Glen Equestrian Park. Sponsored by Jackson County, the park offers picnicking, restrooms, and corrals.

48.5 miles:
Turn left onto Hyatt Prairie Road, traveling toward Hyatt Lake and Hyatt Prairie Lake.

50.4 miles:
Grizzly Campground. A fee area sponsored by Jackson County.

51.9 miles:
Howard Prairie Lake Recreation Site entrance.

53.4 miles:
Keep right on Hyatt Prairie Road.

55.1 miles:
Hyatt Lake comes into view (to the left).

55.9 miles:
Table Mountain Winter Play Area access.

57.3 miles:
Wildlife Viewing Area. Lakeside parking and picnic tables.

57.7 miles:
Lodges. Lakeside parking and picnicking.

59.1 miles:
Turn right onto E. Hyatt Lake Road and travel towards Ashland and Greensprings Highway (to the immediate left at this intersection is access to Hyatt Lake Recreation Area). The E. Hyatt Lake roadway is paved but not striped.

60.6 miles:
Cascade Siskiyou National Monument access on North Chinquapin Mountain Loop Road.

61.7 miles:
Cascade Siskiyou National Monument access on North Chinquapin Mountain Loop Road.

62.0 miles:
Greensprings. The name reflects the perennial green color of the area near the summit of the mountain. At the stop sign, turn left onto Highway 66 and travel toward Keno. Immediately across Highway 66 is the Greensprings Inn and Cabins, a once-important and still popular destination for travelers en route to Crater Lake. From this point, all the way to Worden, the route follows Jesse Applegate's California Trail.

Points En Route continues on next page.

Hyatt Lake

Fort Klamath to Keno (continued)

63.6 miles:
Tub Springs State Park. Picnic area, restrooms, water. At Tub Springs - often-misspelled 'Tubb' Springs - pioneer women washed clothes. The springs were conveniently located close to the trail.

65.4 miles:
Department of Forestry, Lincoln Guard Station.

65.7 miles:
State Highway Maintenance Station.

66.0 miles:
Site of Pinehurst and the location of the old Pinehurst School. Located on the Green Springs Highway, Pinehurst gets its name from the pine trees that grow here and the Old-English word *hurst*, which refers to a wooded eminence, or woods. The post office opened in 1878 and closed in 1882. It reopened as Shake in 1886, and operated until 1911 when the name was changed back to Pinehurst. The Pinehurst economy was dependent on the manufacture of dimension lumber and roof and siding shakes. Pinehurst is located on the Applegate Trail. The old school opened in 1908 and is on the Historic Registry.

66.7 miles:
Mt. View Christian Academy and Church.

66.8 miles:
Mt. View Store and Station. Now closed.

67.4 miles:
The Box R-6 Ranch and Museum.

67.8 miles:
Pinehurst Inn B&B. This 1920s roadhouse inn, located on the historic Applegate Trail, was restored and transformed into a bed and breakfast.

72.3 miles:
Entering Klamath County.

Pinehurst School

Pinehurst Inn

73.1 miles:
Parker Mountain Pass Summit. Elevation: 4356 feet.

74.8 miles:
Unique wooden water tower structure.

82.2 miles:
Hayden Mountain Pass Summit. Elevation: 4695 feet.

86.5 miles:
Upper Klamath Wild and Scenic River access road.

88.0 miles:
Crossing Klamath River.

88.3 miles:
Applegate Trail Historical Marker and Topsy Recreational Site. The first travelers crossed the Klamath River eight miles upstream from this point on October 4, 1846. The route changed in 1847, and the crossing moved to a location less than one-half mile from this point. This is also the 1866 site of Brown's Ferry.

88.8 miles:
Klamath Sportsman's Park, a fee use area.

93.5 miles:
Keno Recreation Area. Camping and RV.

93.9 miles:
Keno

Mt. View Christian Academy and Church

Keno

Elevation: 4108 feet

Location:
42.07.541 N • 121.55.929 W

Services:
gas, food

Keno has a most confusing history! Located on the actual Applegate Trail, the first post office opened in 1876 under the name Whittles Ferry. When the community was first settled, a ferry operated where the bridge is now located, hauling passengers and livestock across the river. The Whittles Ferry Post Office became the Klamath River Post Office and, for a short amount of time, the community was known as Doten. However, confusion with the name Dayton made it a temporary identity, and the Doten Post Office became Plevna, which was also short-lived because it was too difficult to say and spell. The moniker finally became Keno in 1887, after the name given to Captain D.J. Ferree's bird-dog. Ferree was an officer stationed in the area. It is likely that few Oregonians recognize the name Keno even though its population is more than 3000. Well-known to more people, Henley High School - traditionally an athletic powerhouse – is located here.

Whoa Tavern

Former Keno School

Points of Interest

- **Keno Cemetery**
  (Keno-Worden Road and Foley Lane)
  Dates to the 1930s.

- **Keno Ferry Site** *(Greensprings Road/Highway 66 and Park)*
  A ferry operated where the bridge now stands.

- **Keno General Merchandise Store** *(15402 Greensprings Road/Highway 66)*
  The 1920s building is now home to Susie's Archery and Piano Service.

- **Keno Garage** *(15430 Greensprings Road/Highway 66)*
  Formerly a 1940s gas station.

- **Whoa Tavern** *(15468 Greensprings Road/Highway 66)*
  Operating since 1932.

Keno to Klamath Falls

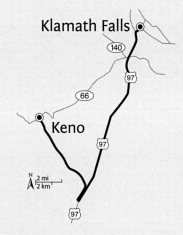

Distance:
  21.0 miles

Directions:
  From the Keno Cemetery, go southeast on Keno-Worden Road.

Points En Route

(mileage from the intersection of Keno-Worden Road and White Goose Road near the cemetery)

0.7 miles:
  St. Pius Catholic Church.

6.9 miles:
  Large grain storage facility.

7.2 miles:
  Bear Valley Eagle Refuge access road. The refuge dates to 1908.

7.3 miles:
  Stop sign. Turn left onto Highway 97, heading toward Klamath Falls.

7.8 miles:
  Worden. The community and post office were named for William Worden, a member of the first group of pioneers who settled in the area and who laid out the town site. At the time, Southern Pacific was building a railroad through the area and Worden acted as the agent who secured much of the needed ground to lay the tracks. The Worden Post Office opened in 1910 but the small town has never incorporated.

13.9 miles:
  Midland Rest Area.

14.0 miles:
  Midland. Midland was platted in 1908 and named because it was, supposedly, mid-way between Portland and San Francisco (it actually is not). The Midland Post Office opened in 1909. At one time, Midland had a livery stable, hotel, saloon, two general stores, and was an important shipping depot. Little remains of the once-thriving community. Carl Banks, a Walt Disney Studios illustrator, is from Midland.

16.4 miles:
  Klamath Wildlife Refuge access road.

17.2 miles:
  Kingsley Field Air Station, an important WWII naval training station.

20.9 miles:
  Exit right off of Highway 97, toward Klamath Falls City Center and Business District.

21.0 miles:
  Klamath Falls

Klamath River near Keno

Klamath Falls

Elevation: 4099 feet

Location:
42.15.054 N • 121.47.271 W

Services:
gas, food, lodging, RV

For thousands of years, the area around Klamath Falls was home to the Modocs, who resented intrusion and land takeover by white settlers. Tension between the two groups began when the Applegate Trail was blazed through this area in 1846. The first known permanent settler was George Nurse, who homesteaded on the Link River in 1867. A small community called Linkville grew and added to problems between settlers and Native Americans. As a result, the 1872-73 Modoc War took place. The war was an expensive campaign for the United States and its cavalry, costing over $8,000,000 in today's money. Seventeen Native Americans and eighty-three soldiers were killed during the two-year skirmish. The Linkville community began to grow and, in 1892, the name was officially changed to Klamath Falls, after the Native Americans who first inhabited the area. The town slowly developed until the early 1900s when marshes and swamps were drained to make the land tillable. The Southern Pacific Railroad laid track through town in 1909, which opened up trade and commerce, and the town quickly grew from a couple hundred people to more than a thousand. A 1920 fire destroyed many of the downtown businesses. As white pine and fir trees were harvested, mills sprang up, and the town flourished. The mills died in the 1980s, a result of both over-harvesting timber and environmentalists' efforts to save the endangered spotted owl. An earthquake in 1993 did considerable damage to the downtown area, including the Courthouse and the Sacred Heart Academy and Convent. Sadly, two deaths resulted from the terrible quake. Water and water rights are the biggest issue facing this southern Oregon community of more than 20,000 people. Balancing water rights and needs of farmers, recreational activities, and endangered species of fish is a politically complicated, delicate process. A dam, built in 2004, has helped resolve some of the tension. The oldest part of the city is located above geothermal hot springs used to heat homes and businesses in the downtown core area. Almost a dozen murals that depict important events in Klamath Falls history are located throughout the community. Rotorua, New Zealand is sister city to Klamath Falls.

Goeller House

Points of Interest

- **Goeller House** (*234 Riverside*)
  A 1905 Victorian.

- **Klamath Visitors Center**
  (*205 Riverside*)
  Knowledgeable staff, lots of information and brochures.

- **Winthrow House** (*204 Riverside*)
  Early 1900s, Colonial Revival construction.

- **Moore House** (*128 Riverside*)
  Built in 1904 for the owners of the first sawmill in town.

- **Veterans Park**
  (*downtown on the water*)
  Locomotive 2579, commissioned in the early 1900s and weighing over 400,000 pounds, is located in the center of the park that overlooks Klamath Lake.

- **Ancient Order of United Workmen** (*25 Main*)
One of only several in the state, the AOUW is a branch of the Masonic Lodge. The building dates to 1899. The Baldwin Hardware Store did business downstairs and the AOUW met upstairs.

- **Baldwin Hotel** (*31 Main*)
Built about 1906, it opened as a hardware store and was converted to a hotel in 1911. Today, it serves as a museum.

- **Flavel Museum** (*125 Main*)
Lots of Native American artifacts and history.

- **Van Fleet Building** (*200 Main*)
Originally the Klamath Falls Women's Library Club building, constructed of locally quarried stone in 1905.

- **Courthouse Annex** (*305 Main*)
Formerly the Elks Temple, the city purchased the building in 1967 after the BPOE abandoned it.

- **Klamath County Courthouse** (*316 Main*)
Built on the site of the 1918 courthouse that was destroyed by the 1993 earthquake.

- **Willits Building** (*430 Main*)
Constructed in 1910 by L.F. Willits, First National Bank president.

- **IOOF Building** (*436 Main*)
1910.

- **Collins Building** (*501 Main*)
A 1919 hotel.

Baldwin Hotel

Courthouse Annex

- **Williams Building** (*724 Main*)
This office building was constructed in 1927 by a cattle baron.

- **JC Penney Building** (*803 Main*)
The building opened in 1928 and became a Penney store in 1937.

- **Oregon Bank Building** (*905 Main*)
Built in 1925, it was linked by tunnels to the Arcade Hotel.

- **Arcade Hotel** (*1032 Main*)
Completed in 1919.

- **Winema Hotel** (*1111 Main*)
This Art Deco style hotel was built in 1930.

- **Klamath Falls City Hall** (*226 5th*)
Built in 1914 and now an apartment building.

- **Klamath County Administration Building** (*500 Klamath*)
Constructed in 1916 as the first city library.

- **Klamath County Museum and Historical Society** (*1451 Main*)
Built in 1935.

- **Linkville Cemetery** (*Upham and East*)
More than one lawman is buried in this 100-year-old cemetery.

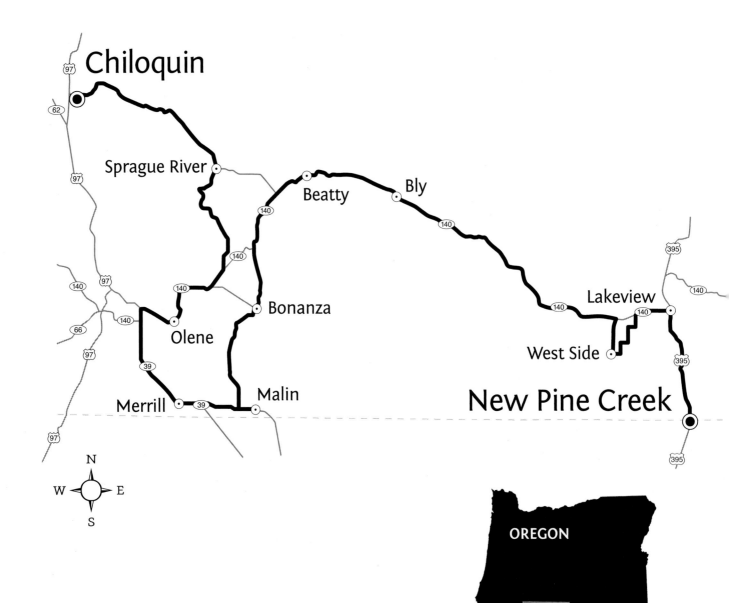

Chiloquin to New Pine Creek

A WWII Bomb, Westside Story, and Oregon's Geyser

Chiloquin to New Pine Creek (195 miles)

Chiloquin was named for a Klamath Indian Chief. Located near the junction of the Williamson and Sprague Rivers, this former timber-dependent town with a once rowdy reputation is making a small resurgence in population, although high unemployment and many vacant homes and businesses exist. From Chiloquin, the route continues to Sprague River, where John C. Fremont and legendary Kit Carson were the first whites to explore the area.

Much geothermal activity, including hot springs, exists in the area. A company recently spent more than $6 million in the Olene area, trying to tap into the abundant hot water that lies beneath the ground. Casualties of a WWII balloon bomb are honored near the small town of Bly. While picnicking, an unsuspecting family investigated the unusual device and became the only people killed on continental United States soil during the war.

Next en route is the small community of West Side. Make sure to visit the old store and photograph the 1916 school teacherage. While in Lakeview, walk the historic downtown core area and visit the old railroad depot before heading out of town to view Oregon's only geyser that erupts about every minute, shooting water up to sixty feet in the air.

The trip concludes in New Pine Creek, a community that bloomed on the Oregon-California border. Here, State Line Road leads to a state park built on the shore of Goose Lake, a very large body of water that mostly lies in California. Make sure to visit the more than 135-year-old gristmill and the 100-year-old church.

Weathered barn near New Pine Creek

Chiloquin

Elevation: 4178 feet

Location:
42.34.562 N • 121.51.794 W
To reach Chiloquin, take exit 247 off Highway 97.

Services:
gas, food, lodging

While Native Americans lived in the area for hundreds of years, Peter Skene Ogden is thought to be the first white person to explore here in 1826. Chiloquin was the pioneer spelling of the spoken word *Chaloquin*, the name of a Klamath Indian Chief whose people lived in the area in the mid 1850s. In 1864, the Klamath Reservation was created, followed by the 1872 Modoc Wars.

Gienger Building

Before the 1920s, Chiloquin was a Native American trading post that consisted of a hotel, livery stable, and store. The railroad came to Chiloquin in 1910, and in 1912, the post office, a mercantile, a warehouse, and the train station opened. The Chiloquin Dam was built in 1914 and removed in 2007. A one-room school was built in 1918 and was big enough for two teachers. The local paper, *Chiloquin Review*, first published news in 1925. The lumber industry gave the town, that incorporated in 1926, its boom. Three mills and a box factory were fully operational that year. The first bank opened in 1927 and was located on Main Street. In 1928, the town was platted, and the library – situated in the City Council Chambers - opened its doors. A 1930 fire destroyed many of the old wooden buildings in the downtown core area. Known for its rowdiness, Chiloquin was referred to as 'Little Chicago.' The town's Train Mountain Miniature Railroad, reportedly the longest in the United States, boasts twenty-five miles of seven and one-half-gauge track. The Williamson and Sprague rivers that join near town offer excellent fishing. Scout Kit Carson was involved in a battle with local Native Americans near here in the 1840s. Chiloquin is a key settlement on the Klamath Reservation. Chiloquin has a state airport, which opened in 1939. Many of the streets in town are Klamath and Modoc tribal names. Edward Chiloquin, born in 1924, is the town's folk hero. A descendent of the Klamath Chief (for whom the town is named), Edward served in World War II and distinguished himself by earning the Silver Star, Bronze Star, Purple Heart with an Oak Cluster, two Asian Pacific Campaign Medals, an Arrowhead, Combat Infantry Badge, and several other medals, ribbons, and badges.

Points of Interest

- **Williamson River**
  Flows through the city center and joins the Sprague River south of town.

- **Friendship Cemetery**
  (Schonchin and Valley)
  1882.

- **Gienger Building** *(117 1st)*
  Constructed between 1923 and 1926. A fire on Thanksgiving in 1955 reduced the grocery/mercantile store to one-story. Apartments filled the second floor.

Hirvi Building

- **Former Chiloquin Post Office**
  (*129 1st*)
  Built in the late 1920s, the
  building has also been home to a
  restaurant, pool hall, and a café.

- **City Park** (*1st and Schonchin*)
  Middle of town.

- **Chiloquin Ice House**
  (*120 Chocktoot*)
  The old building is being
  renovated.

- **Hirvi Building**
  (*1st and Chocktoot*)
  The 1929 building has housed a
  mercantile, the bank, and Safeway.

- **Car Dealership**
  (*1st and Chocktoot – directly across
  from the Hirvi Building*)
  The 8000 square-foot building
  opened in the late 1920s.

- **Clyde's Market** (*1st and Chocktoot
  – diagonally across the intersection
  from the Hirvi Building*)
  The building has undergone major
  changes since it opened in 1937.
  Today it is a gas station.

- **Train Mountain Miniature
  Railroad** (*36941 S Chiloquin Road*)
  The miniature railroad began
  operation in 1975 and is now open
  most Saturdays. The Guinness
  Book of World Records lists it as
  the longest in the US.

- **Chiloquin School**
  Opened in 1963.

Collier Memorial State Park and Logging Museum

- **Collier Memorial State Park
  and Logging Museum**
  (*4600 Highway 97*)
  The museum that opened in
  1945 is located north of the
  community. A 702-year-old
  Douglas fir, toppled during the
  1962 Columbus Day Storm,
  was brought here from Seaside.
  Brothers Andrew and Alfred
  Collier, who donated the land to
  the state, established the park.

- **Kla-Mo-Ya Casino**
  (*34333 Highway 97*)
  Operated by Klamath, Modoc,
  and Yahooskin (Snake Paiute)
  Indians. The casino is located
  south of town.

Chiloquin to Sprague River

Distance:
23.9 miles

Directions:
From the intersection of N 1st Avenue and E Chocktoot Street, drive north on N 1st toward Sprague River. The road is known as Sprague River Road or County Road 858.

Points En Route

(mileage from the intersection of N 1st and E Chocktoot)

0.2 miles:
Williams River and Sprague River conjoin.

2.1 miles:
Sprague River is adjacent to the highway.

3.6 miles:
Abandoned site of one of three original mills in the Chiloquin area.

8.1 miles:
Chiloquin Agency RFD building.

9.8 miles:
Saddle Mountain Peak to the right.

11.1 miles:
Crossing the Sprague River.

11.6 miles:
Potter's Park. Tule Room Store with camping and RV hook-ups.

12.1 miles:
Road parallels the river.

13.9 miles:
Entering Winema National Forest.

14.6 miles:
A dilapidated, stone house.

18.4 miles:
A series of buttes ahead.

20.9 miles:
Eagle Butte Ranch.

23.4 miles:
Public fishing area with pit toilets.

23.9 miles:
Sprague River

Chiloquin

Sprague River

Sprague River storefronts

Sprague River

Elevation: 4365 feet

Location:
42.27.180 N • 121.30.256 W

Services:
gas, food

Native Americans called the Sprague River *Plai* or *Plaikni Koke*, meaning *'a stream that came from higher country.'* The first white men to come to the area were probably John C. Fremont and Kit Carson. Today, the community of Sprague River is aptly named for the river that runs through it. The river itself was named after Captain Franklin B. Sprague, who had a major role in the Snake and Paiute Indian Wars and commanded Fort Klamath in 1866. Sprague River, the youngest community in the Sprague River Valley, has not yet incorporated even though the post office opened in 1923. This office (including the building) was actually moved to this location from Yainax and then, in 1927, was moved from the Yainax building to a location on the ground floor of a rooming house. In 1938, postmaster Anna Wolford moved the office back to its original location. That office closed in 1965 but has re-opened at its current location. A lumber mill opened in 1925 and a box factory opened shortly after. The first school was built in 1923, then another in 1938 that closed around 1964. Long dismantled, the school buildings stood at the corner of Main and 3rd. During Sprague River's heyday, a garage and service station, general store, shoe store and cobbler, restaurant, motel, bakery, drug store, barbershop, pool hall, and confectionary existed. Telephone service came to town in about 1907 and electricity arrived in 1929. The OC&E Railroad (Oregon-California and Eastern) line ran near here in 1928, and today, with tracks removed, forms part of the one-hundred mile Woods Line Nature Trail.

Sprague River Friends Church

Points of Interest

- **Community Center**
  (23536 Main)
  Hub of Sprague River activity.

- **Post Office** *(23415 Main)*
  In a building with the library and Hitchin' Post.

- **Sprague River Library**
  (23415 Main)
  Part of the city block complex that also houses the post office and Hitchin' Post.

- **Palamino General Store**
  (42620 Main)
  1934.

- **Beatty Valley Gospel Mission**
  (42726 Highway 140)
  Dates to the 1930s.

- **Sprague River Park**
  (adjacent to the church property)
  A small park with a playground and barbecues.

- **Nimrod County Park**
  (Moda Street)
  Fishing, pit toilets, picnicking.

- **Chief Schonchin Cemetery**
  (35117 Sprague River Road)
  8.1 miles from town near the intersection of Sprague River Road and Highway 140.

Sprague River to Olene

Distance:
28.8 miles

Directions:
From the Library/Post Office at 1st and Main, drive south on Main Street toward Dairy.

Points En Route

(mileage from the library)

0.2 miles:
Turn right onto Bliss Road.

2.3 miles:
Entering Winema National Forest.

4.2 miles:
OC&E (Oregon, California and Eastern Railroad) State Park. The tracks were removed, providing a 100-mile trail for hikers and bikers to enjoy.

6.8 miles:
Leaving Winema National Forest.

11.7 miles:
Land was cleared here for alfalfa and hay pastures.

14.6 miles:
Abandoned homestead.

16.6 miles:
Turn right onto Highway 140.

16.7 miles:
The 1908 Yonna Valley Store (24985 Highway 140). Originally known as Alkali Valley, the name was changed to *Yonna*, a Native American word for *'below or low down,'* referring to the lower elevation of the area. At one time a post office existed here. The building was moved to this location many years ago.

19.3 miles:
Dairy, settled by William Roberts in 1865, is named after the eastern United States community where Roberts formerly lived. The Dairy Post Office opened in 1876 with Roberts serving as the first postmaster. In 2001, Squaw Flat Road was renamed Bliss Road, after longtime Yonna General Store proprietor David Bliss. Many similar names across the state have been changed because they were offensive and derogatory to Native Americans.

20.5 miles:
Fox Den Ranch. A large buckboard wagon sits near the ranch entrance.

22.2 miles:
Yainax Butte, 7226 feet. *Yainax* is a Klamath Indian word meaning *'little hill.'* The name is applied to both a mountain and the butte. A community by the same name existed near the base of the mountain.

26.2 miles:
Entering the Klamath Reclamation Project area.

27.2 miles:
Stevenson Park. Fishing, picnicking, pit toilets.

28.8 miles:
Olene

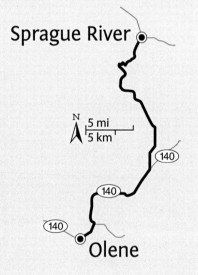

Olene

Elevation: 4128 feet

Location:
42.10.233 N • 121.37.625 W

Services:
gas, food

The name Olene comes from a Klamath term that means *'eddy'* or *'drift place,'* and refers to a location on the river. The Olene Post Office opened in 1884 and closed in 1966. Olene experienced a slight boom in 1918 when the OC&E railroad came through. However, this small, rural, dairy and farming community has never incorporated. The pile of rubble, adjacent to the parking lot near the OC&E Trail marker, is what remains of the old school house. By 2012, Klamath Basin Geopower (KBG) invested more than six million dollars drilling geothermal wells here. The corporation hopes to find enough hot water to build five twenty-megawatt powerhouses by late 2013. Each megawatt of power can bring electricity to 1000 homes.

Points of Interest

- **Olene Store**
  Built circa 1918.

- **OC&E Trail** *(across from the store)*
  Rail lines, now gone, were laid here in 1917. The depot was removed long ago.

- **Olene Hot Springs**
  (North of town on Poe Road)
  The hot water empties into a half-submerged boat where people can sit in the therapeutic waters.

Olene Store

Lost-River Grange

Olene to Merrill

Distance:
17.5 miles

Directions:
From the Olene General Store, drive west on Highway 140.

Points En Route

(mileage from the Olene Store)

0.1 miles:
Lost River Grange #846. The old grange hall building once served as the schoolhouse.

2.1 miles:
Mt. Calvary Catholic Cemetery.

2.6 miles:
Shield Crest Golf Course and Klamath Falls suburban housing development.

4.0 miles:
Intersection with Highway 39. Turn left onto Highway 39 toward Merrill.

4.2 miles:
Klamath Community College.

4.3 miles:
OC&E State Park and linear trail.

4.9 miles:
Eternal Hills Memorial Garden Cemetery.

6.9 miles:
Henley Schools complex.

7.8 miles:
Lost River diversion channel.

9.7 miles:
Mac's Store. The old, 1912 Mt. Laki school sits directly behind the store.

9.8 miles:
Mt. Laki Community Presbyterian Church.

15.0 miles:
An IOOF Cemetery is 0.6 miles to the right. The cemetery dates to the 1920s.

15.7 miles:
Klamath Basin Wildlife Refuge.

17.3 miles:
Mt. Shasta in the distance.

17.5 miles:
Merrill

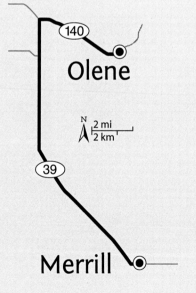

Merrill

Elevation: 4071 feet

Location:
42.01.435 N • 121.36.196 W

Services:
gas, food, lodging

Merrill was named for 1890s settler Nathan S. Merrill, who came from New Hampshire. Merrill bought a ranch here in 1894 and laid out the town. The town incorporated in 1903, and today has a population of about 900 residents. The citizens of Merrill are presently engaged in a 'water war,' as they try to balance finite water resources with the infinite needs and wants of farmers, recreationists, and environmentalists. An annual Potato Festival is held each September.

Points of Interest

- **Merrill IOOF Hall**
  (129 W Front)
  Constructed around 1910.

- **Merrill Bank** *(107 E Front)*
  Built in 1907.

- **Wooden Grain Elevator**
  (3rd and N Washington)
  Few wooden grain elevators exist today because they are susceptible to spontaneous combustion.

- **Merrill Fire Hall** *(Main)*
  The old, four-bay fire hall was replaced in the 1970s.

- **Old House** *(530 E Front)*
  One of the nicest in town; dates to the early 1900s.

- **Old House** *(22505 Front)*
  Neglected, but a beauty in its day.

- **Old House** *(135 Washington)*
  Built around 1916.

Merrill IOOF Hall

- **Merrill Park and Civic Center**
  (Front)
  Formerly the 1915 school.

- **County Cork Collectibles**
  (14141 Falvey Road)
  Located in a 100-year-old farmhouse.

Old House

Wooden Grain Elevator

Merrill Park Civic Center

Malin

Elevation: 4058 feet

Location:
42.00.610 N • 121.24.481 W

Services:
gas, food

Malin is located on the Applegate Trail. In 1872, three families established a cattle ranch in the area, creating friction with the Modoc Indians who, subsequently, killed all of the men on the newly formed ranch. The widows of those killed were anxious to sell the property resulting in a quick sale of the cattle ranch. By 1905, the new owner had constructed a sophisticated irrigation system that was instrumental in bringing other settlers to the area. The burgeoning community, that included a large number of Czech immigrants, was formed in 1909, and a mill and recreation hall were built the next year. Growth was slow but steady, and the town incorporated in 1922, the same year that water, sewer, and electrical services became available. A cheese factory opened in 1923, and a modern mill was built in 1926 to replace the older, smaller one. The railroad came through in the early 1930s, sparking more growth. Potatoes were planted and quickly became the most important cash crop. Today, many of the harvested potatoes are made into potato chips.

Merrill to Malin

Distance:
9.7 miles

Directions:
At the intersection of West Front (Highway 39) and South Garfield, drive east on West Front toward Malin.

Points En Route

(mileage from the Merrill Park Civic Center)

0.2 miles:
St. Augustine Catholic Church (905 E Front).

0.9 miles:
Victorian farmhouse.

2.7 miles:
Turn left onto Highway 50, traveling toward Malin.

2.9 miles:
Stone foundation of a two-story outbuilding.

3.7 miles:
Railroad underpass.

4.4 miles:
Weathered barn, near collapse.

5.3 miles:
Lost River High School.

8.2 miles:
Harpold Road (travelers will come back to this point en route to Bonanza after visiting Malin).

8.5 miles:
Weathered and abandoned farmhouse.

9.6 miles:
Old, photo-worthy, dairy barn.

9.7 miles:
Malin

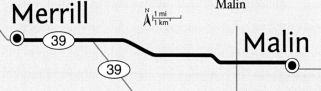

Malin City Park

In 1937, turkey production skyrocketed, and the Malin Cheese Factory was producing more than 650,000 pounds of cheese per year. The small dance hall was replaced, and big name bands such as Lawrence Welk, the Dorsey Brothers, and Wayne King made frequent appearances. In 1925, a major fossil discovery was made just outside of town. Today, a large, thirty-six acre city park, complete with an Olympic size pool and playground, is the town's main attraction. Malin hosts a major car show every 4th of July. Water rights are a major issue in this small, seemingly peaceful community. Farmers, Native Americans, foresters, watershed managers, wildlife managers, and recreational users dispute ownership and use of the area's finite water resources. The US Bureau of Reclamation issued water rights to groups that have exceeded the sustainable capacity. The fertile but sandy soil of Oregon's high desert requires extra water to grow crops. Complicating this issue is the Klamath County Federal Irrigation Project, which was underway prior to 1902, and the 1902 Reclamation Act that granted homestead and water rights in perpetuity to settlers. Too little water plus too many needs and too many interested parties equals an ongoing problem.

Broadway Theater

Malin Drug Store

Points of Interest

- **Malin City Park**
  The city and the BPA operate the large, excellently-maintained park cooperatively. On site are a swimming pool, picnic area, playground equipment, restrooms, and ball fields.

- **Malin Presbyterian Church**
  (2302 5th)
  1924.

- **Broadway Theater** *(2110 Main)*
  The ticket booth and marquee still exist.

- **Malin General Store** *(2115 Main)*
  Opened as a general store but has been Kalina's Hardware for many years.

- **Malin Roller Rink** *(2120 Main)*
  The old roller skating palace is now home to The Way Ministries.

- **Malin Drug Store** *(2139 Main)*
  The original store, complete with a soda fountain and stools, is now home to the historical society.

- **Old Gas Station** *(2217 Broadway)*
  Dates to the 1940s and now an auto repair business.

- **Santford Meats and Groceries** *(2311 Broadway)*
  Built of brick in the 1920s.

- **Malin Cemetery**
  (0.5 miles on Cemetery Road)
  Dates to 1910.

Malin to Bonanza

Distance:
16.5 miles

Directions:
From the Malin Community Park entrance at the west end of town, backtrack on Highway 50 to Harpold Road.

Points En Route

(mileage from Malin Community Park)

1.7 miles:
Turn right onto Harpold Road.

5.8 miles:
Juniper and sagebrush return in the landscape as the road climbs into the hills.

6.6 miles:
Summit with scenic valley views.

9.3 miles:
Very old wooden water tower behind a mobile home.

9.8 miles:
Rajnus Brothers Seed Potatoes. The Rajnus brothers have farmed the area since 1909.

9.9 miles:
Bedfield Cemetery, dates to the early 1900s.

12.4 miles:
Lost River to the left.

13.2 miles:
Intersection with Poe Valley Road. Keep right on Harpold Road towards Bonanza.

14.0 miles:
TransCanada GTN System Compressor Station.

15.0 miles:
Stone manse.

15.1 miles:
Bonanza View Dairy.

15.7 miles:
Keep left on Harpold Road.

16.5 miles:
Bonanza

Bonanza

Elevation: 4199 feet

Location:
42.11.452 N • 121.24.147 W

Services:
gas, food, RV

Bonanza is Spanish for *'prosperity.'* Early settlers, who considered water a source of prosperity, found a 'bonanza' of natural springs in the area and so named the community. Some people say the name came from a successful mining operation that ran from 1877 to 1910, providing an economic 'bonanza' to the area. The town incorporated in 1901. A series of fires destroyed most of the old business and some of the older homes. The Lost River runs through town and, unfortunately, the volume of water has diminished over the past fifty years. Water, once in abundant supply, is a dwindling commodity, pitting environmentalists against farmers over water rights and usage. Bonanza was the setting of the 2011 National Chili Cook-off, held in Big Springs Park.

Points of Interest

- **Bonanza Town Hall** *(2900 4th)*
  A newer modular unit.

- **Bonanza United Methodist Church** *(31897 Mission)*
  Methodists built this church in the 1920s. Today it is the Living Springs Fellowship.

Potato Shed

Bonanza Jail

- **Big Springs Park** (*3001 Main*)
  Restrooms, picnic area, and playground equipment.

- **Bonanza Jail**
  (*behind the post office*)
  The small, 1890 brick building survived the fires.

- **Gas Station** (*2920 Market*)
  Today a small, convenience store.

- **Bonanza Memorial Cemetery**
  (*3200 North Side Road*)
  Dates to 1882 and is also known as the Lost River Cemetery. The Nichols cabin, home to early pioneers, sits near the cemetery.

Bonanza United Methodist Church

Bonanza to Beatty

Distance:
  20.9 miles

Directions:
  From the Bonanza Post Office at 2899 Market, drive north on Market toward Beatty.

Points En Route

(*mileage from the Bonanza Post Office*)

0.3 miles:
  Keep left.

1.2 miles:
  Old Bonanza Schoolhouse. Dates to 1916.

2.5 miles:
  Lava flow.

7.8 miles:
  Stop. Turn right onto Highway 140.

11.3 miles:
  Summit. Bly Mountain Pass, 5087 feet.

12.9 miles:
  Entering Winema National Forest.

13.9 miles:
  More lava.

14.7 miles:
  Leaving Winema National Forest.

20.9 miles:
  Beatty

Beatty

Elevation: 4376 feet

Location:
42.26.508 N • 121.16.277 W

Services:
food

Beatty is an unincorporated community located at the confluence of the Sycan and Sprague rivers. The town was named for Reverend J.L. Beatty, a missionary who lived among the local Native Americans at the turn of the 20th century. In 1908, missionaries Mr. and Mrs. Heffley built the first home in town. The first store opened in the woodshed of the church parsonage, about 1912. The next year, the Beatty Post Office opened in the parsonage. Both burned in 1929 and the post office has been relocated several times since. The first school opened in 1913 and was located about two miles out of town. The building that replaced it in 1925 burned in 1959. Beatty has been plagued with fires that destroyed most of the original homes and businesses in the community.

Beatty School House

Points of Interest

- **Beatty School House** (*Highway 140 and Godawa Springs Road*) 1940.

- **Beatty Store** (*34625 Highway 140*) Built in the 1940s.

- **Masekesket (Brown) Cemetery** (*east of town off Highway 140*) Dates to the 1910s. Toby 'Winema' Riddle is buried here. Riddle was influential in bringing peace between white settlers and Modocs. The cemetery can be seen across the river but is not easily accessible. From Highway 140, go north on Godawa Springs Road about 2.5 miles to the intersection of Sycan Road. Travel on Sycan Road and make a right turn onto Ferguson Road (the sign may not be there). Keep bearing right and soon the road will turn into a one-lane road. Follow this road until you come to a crest before dropping down toward the Sprague River. Follow the left track and the road will lead you to the cemetery.

Beatty to Bly

Distance:
12.2 miles

Directions:
From the Beatty (Palamino) Store and Deli at 34625 Highway 140, drive east on Highway 140 toward Bly.

Points En Route

(mileage from the Beatty Store)

1.3 miles:
Beatty Cemetery can be seen across the river.

3.6 miles:
The road parallels the Sprague River. White birch trees line the river.

4.6 miles:
River access. Parking and pit toilets.

7.8 miles:
Lowlands that lie between the Bly Ridge Mountains and a series of buttes.

12.0 miles:
South Fork Trading Post to the left and an abandoned house to the right.

12.2 miles:
Bly

Bly

Elevation: 4330 feet

Location:
42.23.917 N • 121.02.633 W

Services:
gas, food, lodging

The name Bly is an Anglicized version of the Klamath Indian term *p'lai*, which means *'up high.'* Records do not identify the first settlers in the area, but show that emigrant John Gearhardt (for whom the mountains are named) came about 1871. The post office opened in 1873 under the name of Sprague River, then changed to Bly in 1883. The railroad came through and the depot was constructed in 1929.

Bly Ranger Station

Logging became an important industry with much of the timber going to nearby mines. The original cemetery was located at the site of the District Ranger Station, and in 1901, the coffins were relocated three and one-half miles away. The first school opened in 1873, and the building was replaced in 1910. A gym was added in 1921. The 1910 school burned and a new one was constructed in 1932. In 1925, a short-lived range war ended with the death of one farmer and the imprisonment of another, all over ownership of a black sheep. Extensive logging activity took place from 1929 to 1939, when many people moved into the area to find employment in the forests and mills. The first sawmill was built in 1931 and did not close until 1984. In 1932, the school building burned again and was replaced with the current structure. In 1935 the CCC constructed a district ranger station here and the seven original buildings still stand. Oddly, Bly is the site of the only stateside civilian casualties of WWII when, on May 5, 1945, six curious picnickers untangled a balloon from thick brush and the attached bomb exploded. In 2002, federal authorities arrested Earnest James Ujaama (Abu Hamza al-Masri) for crimes against the government when he was indicted on conspiracy to set up a terrorist training camp near here just prior to the 9/11 attacks. Bly, located near the eastern end of the 100-mile-long OC&E Woods Line State Trail, has never incorporated. The local economy is made up of ranching and government-related work.

Points of Interest

- **Bly Ranger Station**
  (Highway 140 and Gerber)
  Seven buildings stand, all constructed by the CCC in the 1930s. This was the original location of the Bly Cemetery. All of the bodies and headstones were moved to the new cemetery before construction of the ranger station.

W.W. Smith Mercantile

Bly

Points of Interest (continued)

- **Star Theater** (*61100 Highway 140*)
  The theater opened in 1948 as Arch Memorial Theater and is now a thrift shop.

- **Christian and Missionary Alliance Church**
  (*61125 Highway 140 E*)
  Circa 1920.

- **W.W. Smith Mercantile**
  (*Highway 140 and Edler*)
  Dates to 1899 when it opened as a trading post.

- **Gearhardt Gym** (*on Edler behind the Assembly of God Church*)
  The old gym was constructed in 1921 and named after early settler John Area Gearhardt.

- **Bly Cemetery**
  1901.

- **Mitchell Recreation**
  (*several miles out of town – see Bly to West Side below at 1.1 miles*)
  Site of the balloon bomb explosion that took the lives of six Bly residents on May 5, 1945.

Star Theater

Gearhardt Gym

Bly to West Side

Distance:
39.4 miles

Directions:
From the intersection of Edler Street and Highway 140 (at Plum Tuckered Out Antique Store), drive east on Highway 140 toward Lakeview.

Points En Route

(mileage from the intersection of Edler Street and Highway 140)

1.1 miles:
Intersection with Campbell Road. The Mitchell Monument Shrapnel Tree is located about nine miles off of Forest Road 34 (0.5 miles from the intersection of Highway 140 and Campbell).

4.2 miles:
Sprague River and Fremont National Forest. Picnic area.

7.4 miles:
A volcanic butte is visible ahead and to the left.

9.4 miles:
Chain up area. Entering Lake County.

12.7 miles:
Lofton Recreation Area access road.

12.7 miles:
Summit. Quartz Mountain, 5504 feet.

12.7 miles:
Quartz Mountain Sno-Park; pit toilets.

15.5 miles:
Quartz Creek.

16.9 miles:
Leaving Fremont-Winema National Forest.

17.7 miles:
Crossing Drews Creek.

18.1 miles:
Drew's Valley.

18.4 miles:
Interpretive marker – Drew's Valley Ranch. Drew's Valley Reservoir is visible in the distance.

19.7 miles:
Drew's Valley Ranch Headquarters.

19.7 miles:
Cottonwood Meadow Lake access road.

23.8 miles:
Old home on the edge of the basin.

24.5 miles:
Drew Reservoir.

27.9 miles:
Drew's Gap Summit, 5306 feet.

29.1 miles:
Booth State Park. Picnic area and pit toilets.

30.7 miles:
Old home, likely a former schoolhouse.

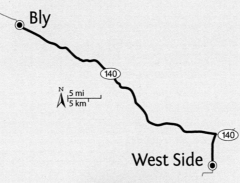

32.4 miles:
Juniper Reservoir RV Resort.

35.0 miles:
Turn right onto Tunnel Hill Road, heading south toward Westside.

37.2 miles:
Weathervane/windmill.

39.0 miles:
Drew's Reservoir and West Side Cemetery access road. The cemetery dates to the early 1900s.

39.4 miles:
West Side

Road between Bly and West Side

West Side

Elevation: 4428 feet

Location:
42.06.796 N • 120.29.611 W

Services:
food

West Side, an unincorporated community, is located on the west side of Goose Lake. The West Side Post Office opened in 1923 and closed in 1942. Many pictographs and petroglyphs are located in the area and the county museum displays many Native American artifacts found locally.

Points of Interest

- **West Side Store**
  Turn of the twentieth century construction.

- **West Side Grange #854**
  Dates to the 1920s.

- **West Side School**
  1919. Originaly named Union School. The two-unit teacherage, located behind the school, dates to 1916.

West Side School

West Side to Lakeview

Distance:
11.2 miles

Directions:
From the intersection of Water User's Lane and West Side Road (at the West Side Store), drive east on Water User's Lane.

Points En Route

(mileage from the West Side General Store)

0.9 miles:
Turn left onto Garrett Road, heading north.

2.2 miles:
Victorian house.

2.5 miles:
Stop. Turn right onto West Side Road, heading east.

3.2 miles:
Old weathervane and windmill.

4.6 miles:
Old log cabin outbuilding.

5.4 miles:
Keep right.

7.9 miles:
Stop sign. Turn right onto Highway 140. This intersection is called 'Five Corners.'

9.0 miles:
Golf course.

10.0 miles:
Airport Road.

10.3 miles:
Crossing Thomas Creek.

10.8 miles:
Crossing Warner Canyon Creek.

11.0 miles:
An old barn, ready to fall.

11.2 miles:
Lakeview

Lakeview

Elevation: 4800 feet

Location:
42.11.676 N • 120.20.802 W

Services:
gas, food, lodging, RV

The first permanent settler in the area was M.W. Bullard, who arrived in 1869. Bullard sold 300 acres to settler John Moon, who suggested the name Lakeview for the growing community. At that time, Goose Lake (which has since greatly receded) could easily be seen from the newly formed town site. The post office opened in 1874, then the town was established in 1876 and incorporated in 1893. The town grew as a commercial center for area cattle and sheep ranches. In 1900, a tragic fire burned almost every home and business in town, sparing only two buildings. The community totally rebuilt within two years and became the Lake County seat. A second fire, in 1906, did considerable damage to many stick-built homes. Businesses made of brick were spared. Sadly, a third fire that occurred in 1916 destroyed most of the homes that survived the 1906 fire. Lakeview is almost one mile high, making it the most elevated municipality in Oregon. A geyser was created in hot springs located here when geothermal well drillers tapped into the 200-degree surface water. In season, the geyser goes off every two to five minutes and can reach heights of sixty feet. Lakeview continues to be a regional business center with lumber and agriculture its main industries.

Lake County Museum

Points of Interest

- **Bank of Lakeview** *(1 South E)*
  Opened in 1898 and survived the fire.

- **Masonic Lodge** *(19 South E)*
  Built after the fire in 1908.

- **Lake County Museum**
  (118 South E)
  Located in the 1927 Albert Kent house, the museum opened in 1991.

- **Schminck Museum**
  (128 South E)
  The original 1922 craftsman home of a pioneer family is now the second museum in town and displays many Native American artifacts.

- **Heryford Building**
  (540 South E)
  Built in 1913. Downstairs was a department store and the Elks Lodge occupied the second floor.

- **Bailey-Massingill Building**
  (4 North E)
  Built in 1900.

- **Rexall Drug Store**
  (North E and 1st)
  1907.

- **Lake County Museum**
  (118 North E)
  Contains lots of interesting information about Lake County.

Lakeview

Points of Interest (continued)

- **Lakeview Bank**
  (120 North E)
  The 1887 bank building now houses a real estate office.

- **Post and King Building**
  (125 North E)
  Opened as a saloon in 1896. In 1901, a dance hall was added to the second story.

- **Lakeview Hardware**
  (126 North E)
  The Chamber of Commerce now occupies the old hardware store building.

- **Wilcox Building**
  (North E and Center)
  The building opened in 1901 as the First National Bank of Portland.

- **IOOF** *(3 South F)*
  Opened in 1911 and restored in 2002.

- **Alger Theater**
  (24 South F)
  Built in the 1930s.

- **Courthouse** *(513 Center)*
  Newer construction.

- **Lakeview United Methodist Church** *(South H and Center)*
  1892.

- **Chandler House**
  (South H and Center)
  A 1905 Queen Anne originally built for J.N. Watson.

- **Nevada/California/Oregon Railroad Depot** *(1400 Center)*
  Built in 1913 and now a private residence.

- **Heryford House** *(1st and F)*
  1913.

Post and King Building

Nevada/California/Oregon Railroad Depot

Conn House

- **Old Warehouse**
  (1st and Lake Place)
  1901.

- **St. Patrick Catholic Church**
  (12 North G)
  1911.

- **Conn House** *(170 S. G)*
  A 1917 Queen Anne.

- **Lakeview Town Hall**
  (525 North 1st)
  The building originally housed the jail, library, fire, and police offices.

- **Lakeview First Baptist Church** *(910 North 2nd)*
  1910.

- **Outdoor Walking Museum**
  (1900 North 4th)
  Located at the fairgrounds. Many old farm implements and other outdoor items are displayed.

- **Lakeview IOOF Cemetery**
  (12th and J)
  1879.

- **Sunset Park Cemetery**
  (North G and Highway 395)
  Dates to 1919 and is also known as the Lakeview Cemetery.

- **Hunters Hot Spring and Lakeview Geyser**
  (18088 Highway 395)
  A lodge motel sits adjacent to the hot springs and geyser that are easily viewed from the parking lot.

Lakeview United Methodist Church

Lakeview Geyser

Lakeview to New Pine Creek

Distance:
14.1 miles

Directions:
From the Lake County Courthouse (Center and F), drive south on F Street to New Pine Creek (note: F Street becomes Highway 395).

Points En Route

(mileage from the Lake County Courthouse)

0.5 miles:
Episcopal Church and adjacent school.

1.3 miles:
Lakeview Interagency Offices; BLM and Department of Forestry.

5.7 miles:
Red Victorian farmhouse. Goose Lake is in the distance.

13.1 miles:
Leaving 'Oregon Outback Country.'

14.1 miles:
New Pine Creek

Victorian house

New Pine Creek

Elevation: 4938 feet

Location:
41.59.591 N • 120.59.885 W

Services:
none

New Pine Creek is uniquely platted on the Oregon/California border and, technically, lies in both states. With the exception of one home, all information and points of interest listed below are on the Oregon side of the community. New Pine Creek, Oregon, is alleged to be the oldest town in Lake County but has never incorporated. The post office opened in 1876 and was named due to its location on Pine Creek. Because the name Pine Creek was already used, postal authorities quickly changed the name to New Pine Creek, avoiding confusion. At just 300 feet short of a mile-high elevation, New Pine Creek averages twelve inches of rain and about thirty inches of snowfall each year, yet averages more than 210 days of sunshine. Thunder eggs, petrified wood, and agates are found north of New Pine.

Points of Interest

- **New Pine Cemetery** (*north of the community off of Highway 395*) 1904.

- **New Pine Mercantile** (*11153 Highway 395*) The 1907 building still bears original signs on its storefront. Today it is 'Just Stuff,' an antique and collectable store.

- **Ben Warner General Store**
(*the garage-type building behind New Pine Mercantile*)
The store was originally established where the mercantile is today and moved to this location in 1907.

- **Shorty's Tavern**
(*across State Line Drive*)
This small, dilapidated building housed a tavern, beginning in 1900.

- **Old Barn** (*north of Shorty's Tavern on State Line Drive*)
Circa 1910.

- **East Side Grange #585**
(*11179 Highway 395*)
Built in 1911 after the fire, the Thomas Building housed the Antler Saloon until 1921 when it was sold to the Grange.

- **Goose Lake First Baptist Church** (*97650 Church Lane*)
Opened in 1887 across the state line in California. The church building was moved to this location on the Oregon side of the border in 1941 and today is known as the New Pine Creek First Baptist Church.

- **Keller House**
(*97806 Church Lane*)
Dates to 1907. Keller once owned the gristmill.

- **New Pine Creek Grist Mill**
(*end of Church – on private property*)
The mill opened in 1871.

East Side Grange

New Pine Creek Grist Mill

- **Goose Lake State Park**
(*State Line Drive*)
The lake is eight miles wide and more than twenty miles long with an average depth of only four feet. The shoreline of this shallow lake provides migratory and nesting areas and affords excellent bird watching.

- **Victorian House**
(*behind the entrance sign on Highway 395 to Goose Lake Park*)
While officially not in Oregon, this old house is worthy of mention. Eli Craven Mason, the first judge in Lake County, built the house in 1880 on the California side of State Line Road.

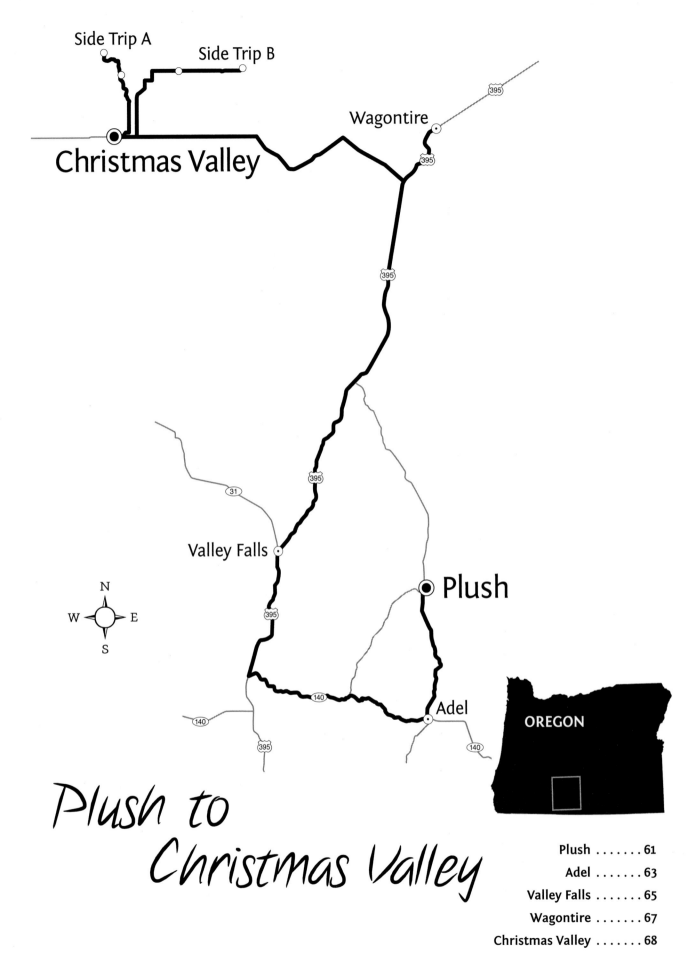

Side Trip A

Side Trip B

Wagontire

395

395

Christmas Valley

395

31

395

Valley Falls

N
W   E
S

Plush

395

140

140

140

Adel

140

OREGON

Plush to
Christmas Valley

Gemstones, Rudolph, and a Crack in the Ground

Plush to Christmas Valley (172 miles)

Sunstones, the Oregon State Gem, can be found in the Plush area at the beginning of this tour that covers more than 170 miles through Oregon's outback, taking travelers by several shallow lakes that are amply stocked with pan fish. Located near Hart Lake and the Antelope Refuge, tiny Plush once boasted a population of 2,000.

From Plush, travel to Adel and its 1897 store, then on into Oregon's Outback and Lake Abert, an alkali body of water. Continue through the outback to Wagontire - Oregon's newest ghost town since the store and gas station closed in 2009. An RV park, located next to the store, is open seasonally. The airstrip is seldom used, especially since the store closed. Locals say pilots landed their planes, taxied to the store for lunch, and then took off, using the highway as a runway.

The route ends in Christmas Valley, a planned 1960s community with street and business names in sync with a Christmas theme. Alternate routes to Crack-in-the-Ground, Sand Dune Recreation Area, and Lost Forest - all worthy of exploration - originate in Christmas Valley.

Hart Mountain near Valley Falls

Plush

Elevation: 4506 feet

Location:
42.24.674 N • 119.54.255 W

Services:
gas, food, limited lodging

Plush is home to the Sunstone, Oregon's state gemstone. These semi-precious gems can be found lying atop the ground. Larger stones, some of which have considerable value, can be dug in several places for a small fee. The Plush area feldspar stones contain copper, which makes them unique to any other sunstones in the world. Plush was named when, during a poker game, a Paiute Nation warrior yelled, "I have a Plush!" In the 1920s, Plush boasted a population of almost 2000 people, and today has a high seasonal count of around eighty inhabitants. The small community has never incorporated.

Plush Community Church

Points of Interest

- **Egan Park**
  (Hogback Road and Warner)
  Picnic, restrooms, playground.

- **Plush Community Hall**
  Center of activity.

- **Plush (Hart Mountain) Store**
  (28229 Hogback)
  Stocks a little bit of everything and also serves as a tavern and eatery.

- **Plush Community Church**
  (Hogback Road and Plush Cut-off Road)
  Non-denominational.

- **Plush School**
  (Warner and Road 3041)
  This newer school replaced the one built in 1929.

- **Antelope Refuge**
  The refuge entrance and park headquarters are located 7.4 miles from Plush on paved road, followed by 16.3 miles of graveled road. Hart Mountain is a massive 8065 foot fault-block ridge that ascends almost three-fourths of a mile above the floor of Warner Valley. Dedicated in 1936, the 276,000-acre refuge is one of the most expansive wildlife habitats in the West. More than 300 species of wildlife have been identified, including big horn sheep, which are frequently spotted. Hart Mountain Hot Springs is 4.3 miles from the park headquarters.

Plush to Adel

Distance:
17.8 miles

Directions:
From the Hart Mountain Store on Plush-Adel Road, drive south on Plush-Adel Road toward Adel.

Points En Route

(mileage from the store)

0.3 miles:
Turn left to stay on Plush-Adel Road.

0.8 miles:
Huge boulders have fallen from the rocky butte. The road passes through Warner Valley.

5.3 miles:
Seasonal lake.

7.2 miles:
View of Crump Lake, known for its bass fishing. The lake went completely dry in the 1950s, revealing many Native American artifacts. During the wet season, the lake can cover more than 1800 acres.

8.9 miles:
L.X. Ranch, 1918.

10.7 miles:
Fischer Lake.

13.1 miles:
More huge boulders.

14.9 miles:
Pelican Lake. Bass fishing.

17.5 miles:
Crump Ranch and 1895 Century House.

17.8 miles:
Adel

Crump Lake

Adel

Elevation: 4588 feet

Location:
42.10.571 N • 119.53.396 W

Services:
gas, food, RV

The earliest settlers here were Catholics from County Cork, Ireland who ranched sheep and cattle and farmed the area near Deep Creek. How Adel was named remains uncertain, with two possible explanations. The first, and most plausible, is that the town was named for early area settler Bert Sessions' sweetheart. Sessions owned the land on which the post office was constructed. A less glamorous and less probable explanation is that Adel was named after a cow named Leda. If the four letters in Leda are rearranged they spell Adel. Regardless, the Adel Post Office opened in 1896. Sunstones are mined locally.

Points of Interest

- **Adel Store**
  1897.

- **Adel School**
  (18286 Twenty Mile Road)
  1929.

- **Adel Cemetery**
  Opened in 1988.

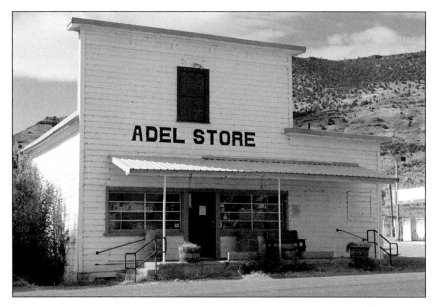

Adel Store

Deep Creek Falls

Valley floor near Valley Falls

Adel to Valley Falls

Distance:
45.2 miles

Directions:
From the Adel Store at the intersection of Highway 140 and Twenty Mile Road, drive west on Highway 140 toward Lakeview.

Points En Route

(mileage from the Adel Store)

0.1 miles:
1988 Adel Cemetery.

0.9 miles:
Diversion dam on Deep Creek.

2.1 miles:
Columnar basalt pillars to the right.

2.7 miles:
Deep Creek Falls. Several pull-outs are available.

3.8 miles:
Abandoned ranch house.

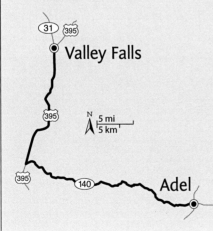

6.0 miles:
The road ascends and Deep Creek disappears to the south.

6.9 miles:
Crossing Drake Creek.

9.6 miles:
Chain-up area. Snow zone in winter.

10.6 miles:
Road narrows.

11.0 miles:
Crane Creek Ranch entrance #1.

12.2 miles:
Plush Mountain and Hart Wildlife Refuge cut-off. Stay straight on Highway 140.

12.6 miles:
Crossing Blue Creek.

14.1 miles:
Crane Creek Ranch entrance #2.

16.3 miles:
Crane Creek Ranch entrance #3.

16.8 miles:
Entering Fremont National Forest.

18.5 miles:
Crossing Bowers Bridge Creek.

19.7 miles:
Willow Creek Campground to the left. Muddy Creek Campground to the right.

22.9 miles:
Warner Pass Summit, 5380 feet.

23.5 miles:
Warner Canyon Ski Area.

25.0 miles:
Leaving Fremont National Forest.

26.2 miles:
A privately owned covered bridge.

27.7 miles:
Stop sign. Turn right onto Highway 395, heading toward Valley Falls.

27.9 miles:
Oregon Outback Scenic Byway marker.

34.0 miles:
Valley floor.

39.0 miles:
Crossing Crooked Creek.

39.9 miles:
Chandler State Park and Scenic Byway kiosk.

42.1 miles:
Old farmhouse.

43.0 miles:
Abert Rim Oasis RV Park.

44.1 miles:
Oregon History Kiosk.

45.2 miles:
Valley Falls

Valley Falls

Elevation: 4327 feet

Location:
42.29.047 N • 120.16.949 W

Services:
gas, food, RV

Located at the southern tip of Abert Lake, Valley Falls is named for a small falls in the Chewaucan River, about one mile north of the community. The Valley Falls Post Office opened in 1909, was moved in 1942, and closed in 1943. Many people come to the area to climb the Abert Rim, a large fault block mountain.

Points of Interest

- **Valley Falls Store**
  (28314 Highway 395)
  Constructed in the 1920s.

- **Lake Abert**
  A large, alkali lake located north of the small community.

Valley Falls Store

Lake Abert

Valley Falls to Wagontire

Distance:
60.6 miles

Directions:
From the Valley Falls Store at the intersection of Highway 31 and Highway 395, drive north on Highway 395 toward Alkali Lake and Burns.

Points En Route

(mileage from the Valley Falls Store)

Note: Next gas is 90 miles.

1.6 miles:
Abert Rim to the right. The rim is more than 2500 feet above the lake and extends almost thirty miles, making it one of the largest fault scarps in the United States. Lake Abert is an important spring and fall stopover for migrating water-birds, including the Northern Shoveler, Canada Snow, and California Gull. In summer, terns, avocets, grebes, ruddy ducks, and stilts can be observed here.

2.0 miles:
A small body of water, connected to Lake Abert during the wet season.

2.8 miles:
Lake Abert, frequently rimmed with a deposit of alkali.

4.8 miles:
Big Horn Sheep warning.

5.6 miles:
Lake Abert wildlife viewing area.

7.7 miles:
Large boulders.

9.0 miles:
Abert Rim Geological Marker. John C. Fremont explored the area in 1843.

18.1 miles:
North end of Lake Abert.

20.4 miles:
The lake shoreline, colored white from alkali deposits, is approximately eighteen miles long.

22.0 miles:
The landscape is totally barren of trees. Hills are covered with sagebrush.

24.2 miles:
Deer fences.

29.1 miles:
Coleman Flats Rest Area. Picnic, restrooms, travel information. The tall peak to the north and west is Juniper Mountain, elevation: 6679 feet.

37.5 miles:
Alkali Lake to the left. Eons ago, the lake had a depth of more than 270 feet and covered almost 1500 square miles.

38.9 miles:
Alkali Lake Station. Located on Highway 395, there is not much to see at this Lake County Maintenance Station. The lake water contains ten percent salt. The wayside is obviously named for the brackish lake water.

42.3 miles:
Sand dune area.

47.9 miles:
Seasonal water on both sides of the highway. This body of water is known as North Alkali Lake.

52.1 miles:
Christmas Valley Junction. Keep straight on Highway 395, traveling toward Wagontire. Note: The route returns to this point after stopping in Wagontire.

54.2 miles:
The peak to the right is Little Juniper Mountain, elevation: 6413 feet.

56.1 miles:
Entering Harney County. The roadway becomes rougher and the landscape remains desolate.

59.6 miles:
Road narrows.

60.6 miles:
Wagontire

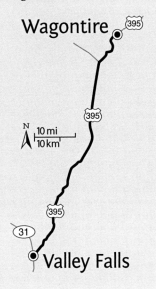

Wagontire

Elevation: 4730 feet

Location:
43.14.980 N • 119.52.600 W

Services:
none

Out of the way and mostly forgotten, Wagontire has become a 21st century ghost town. For many years the total population was two residents who operated the store, café, gas pumps, and RV Park. Named after the 6504 foot Wagontire Mountain, the small community was an oasis to travelers that found themselves in need of gas or groceries. The first settlers in the area were the Egli family, who came about 1900. Their name was given to the ranch and then to the post office. The name was changed to Wagontire, after the mountain, in 1919. The post office, that closed in 1943 and was demolished years ago, was located across the street from the store. Before the store closed, travelers had to be on the alert for aircraft that used Highway 395 as a runway. The highway was sometimes preferred over the nearby dirt airstrip by pilots who landed their aircraft, taxied to the café for lunch, and fueled at the pumps before take-off. Wagontire Mountain is named for a pioneer wagon wheel that was discovered near here. Forty-nine, three-inch cannon balls were also found in 1978 but no one knows their origin.

Bruce Fingerhood

Wagontire Store

Points of Interest

- **Wagontire Store**
  The store dates to the early 1960s, replacing a two-story one.

- **Wagontire Motel**
  Now used by the owner and friends when they hunt.

- **Wagontire RV**
  Open seasonally and by chance.

- **Wagontire Airport**
  Constructed in 1987 by William Warner, owner of Wagontire from 1986 to 1997.

Wagontire to Christmas Valley

Distance:
48.6 miles

Directions:
From the Wagontire Store, return south on Highway 395 (8.6 miles) to the Christmas Valley Junction.

Points En Route

(mileage from the Wagontire Store)

8.6 miles:
Turn right toward Christmas Valley.

9.9 miles:
Cattle guard, one of many en route to Christmas Valley.

12.6 miles:
Oasis Ranch. Irrigated land in the midst of sage and rabbit brush.

15.8 miles:
Open rangeland.

17.0 mils:
An eight-degree ascent.

18.1 miles:
Summit.

18.8 miles:
Chain-up/removal area.

31.0 miles:
Newly constructed, stick-built

Christmas Valley

Elevation: 4321 feet

Location:
43.14.259 N • 120.41.193 W

Services:
gas, food, lodging, RV

The name Christmas Valley is a corruption of the family name Christman, early settlers that came to the area in the 1870s. A post office, under the name of Lake, operated from 1909 to 1943. The Christmas Valley Post Office opened in 1963, when a developer began advertising and selling real estate in this high desert area. The developer was sued for false advertising after he sold almost 5000 parcels of ground, few of which have been built upon. Street names such as Mistletoe Road, Comet Street, and Candy Lane reflect the community's Christmas theme. Many ATV enthusiasts come to Christmas Valley to ride in the dunes area. An airport and landing field parallels the highway that runs through the community. Christmas Valley remains unincorporated.

Points of Interest

- **Christmas Valley Lake**
  Man-made in the late 1960s, the name has been changed to Baert Lake.

- **Christmas Valley Park**
  (*Christmas Valley Highway, between Bay and Park*)
  Picnic area, tennis courts, playground.

- **Christmas Valley Golf Course**
  (*Christmas Tree Lane*)
  The 18-hole course has affordable fees and offers memberships.

Christmas Valley Lake

Christmas Valley   Wagontire

home, a rarity on this thirty-five mile stretch of road. Travel trailers and mobile/manufactured homes dot the landscape every few miles.

35.6 miles:
Utility poles appear suddenly and line the roadway.

38.3 miles:
Large, ranch house.

39.3 miles:
Stick-built house.

39.8 miles:
Solar Power Station: Belectric Company.

40.3 miles:
Alfalfa fields. A brilliant green color in season.

41.7 miles:
Fossil Lake Road. Keep straight.

48.4 miles:
Homes to the left have airplane hangars and windsocks.

47.7 miles:
The access road to Crack-in-the-Ground, Christmas Lake, Sand Dunes, and Lost Forest (optional side-trips).

48.6 miles:
Christmas Valley

Side Trip A – Crack in the Ground and Green Mountain Lookout

Distance:

Crack in the Ground – 7.1 miles
Green Mountain Lookout – 12.0 miles

Directions:

From the east city limits of Christmas Valley at the intersection of Crack in the Ground Road and Christmas Valley Highway, drive north on Crack in the Ground Road. The drive is on a well-maintained gravel road.

Points En Route

(mileage from the intersection of Crack in the Ground Road and Christmas Valley Highway)

4.6 miles:

Cattle guard.

7.1 miles:

Crack in the Ground parking area and pit toilet. From here, hike 0.6 miles to the two fissure entrances. Crack in the Ground

is a volcanic fissure that extends over two miles, is more than seventy feet at its greatest depth, and at one point measures fifty-feet wide. The fissure occurred about one thousand years ago – mere minutes on the geologic time table. Ice is frequently found during summer months in areas along the fissure. In the 1960s, astronauts trained here because of the supposed similarity to the moon's surface.

8.8 miles:

Cattle guard. There is a volcanic crater to the right.

10.3 miles:

Keep left on the graveled portion of the road.

12.0 miles:

Green Mountain Lookout tower access. Green Mountain, the highest point in the area, is 5190 feet.

12.5 miles:

Green Mountain Campground.

Note: The road continues past this point, but at 13.1 miles is not recommended for family cars.

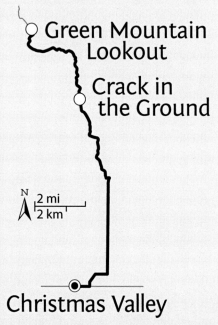

N
2 mi
2 km

Crack in the Ground

Road near Crack in the Ground

Side Trip B – Sand Dunes and Lost Forest

Distance:

Sand Dunes – 17.7 miles
Lost Forest – 22.2 miles

Directions:

From the east entrance to Christmas Valley at the intersection of Christmas Valley Highway and Crack in the Ground Road, drive east on Christmas Valley Highway.

Points En Route

(mileage from the intersection of Christmas Valley Highway and Crack in the Ground Road)

0.9 miles:

Turn left onto Millican Road. This is an Oregon Back Country Byway.

3.9 miles:

B and K Farms and Church Family Farms.

10.7 miles:

Keep right onto Lost Forest Lane.

13.7 miles:

Stone building.

14.4 miles:

Pavement ends. Continue along 3.3 miles of gravel to the Sand Dunes and 7.8 miles to Lost Forest. You are traveling in an ancient lakebed called the Fossil Lake Area, which is closed to off-highway vehicles. The area contains many fossils that range from 10,000- to 400,000-years-old. Hundreds of species of birds, reptiles, fish, and mammals have been discovered. Examples are the mammoth, giant beaver, Dire wolf, and a large eagle. Paleontologists and archeologists have been studying the Fossil Lake area since 1878.

17.7 miles:

Christmas Valley Sand Dunes Recreation Area. Kiosk and sign-in.

17.9 miles:

Entering limited use area. All vehicle use is restricted to posted roads and trails.

21.3 miles:

Junipers Campground access road (dirt road).

21.8 miles:

Dunes and campground access road. Drive at your discretion.

22.0 miles:

Left to Lost Forest.

22.2 miles:

Lost Forest Research Natural Area, elevation: 4400 feet. Roads are not improved and not recommended for low clearance vehicles. Primitive toilets are available, but no water. The Lost Forest consists of 9000 acres of small, ponderosa pine trees, thirty-five miles from the nearest forest. Vehicles are restricted to the roads in order to preserve the forest and its lands. Numerous species of birds, reptiles, and mammals live within the forest habitat.

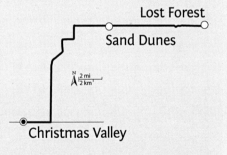

Christmas Valley Sand Dunes

Lost Forest

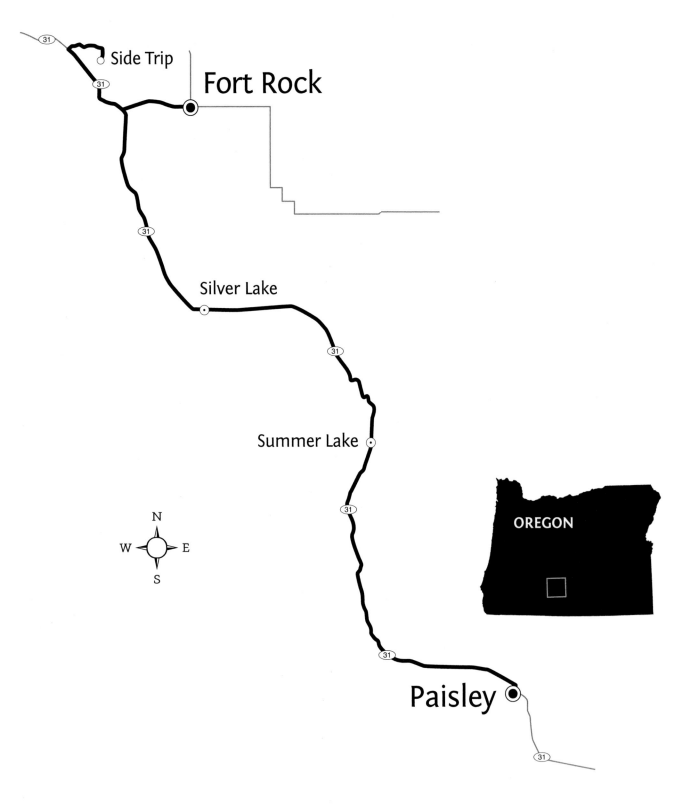

Side Trip

Fort Rock

Silver Lake

Summer Lake

N
W · E
S

OREGON

Paisley

Paisley to Fort Rock

Going from the 70s, Past a Tragic Fire, to a Hole in the Ground

Paisley to Fort Rock (74 miles)

The headquarters of the largest ranch in Oregon – the ZX Ranch – located in Oregon's outback at Paisley, marks the beginning of this route. The word paisley conjures up images of the 1970s: leisure suits, long hair, and paisley print rayon shirts with the droplet-shaped, vegetable motif patterns that originated in Persia. However, this small town on the edge of the Great Basin was named by immigrants from Paisley, Scotland in honor of their homeland – not for the mod print. While in Paisley, enjoy a 'cold one' at the Pioneer Saloon, and admire the 1883 bar, shipped 'round the horn to its current location.

From Paisley, travel past Summer Lake Hot Springs, a natural hot spring area used by Native Americans for centuries. Following discovery by John C. Fremont in 1843, the springs were used by hundreds of settlers, hunters, and travelers until commercialized in the 1920s. From Summer Lake, the tour leads to Silver Lake, a community struck by misfortune. In 1894, in what should have been a festive Christmas celebration, tragedy struck when forty-three people lost their lives in a deadly fire.

Continue north toward Fort Rock, a volcano in the midst of an ancient lakebed and near the location where sandals that are more than 10,000 years old were discovered. From Fort Rock and its historic, open-air museum, take a side trip to Hole in the Ground, a near perfect circular crater, formed more than 15,000 years ago when a volcano erupted.

Road near Hole in the Ground

Paisley

Elevation: 4369 feet

Location:
42.41.573 N • 120.32.395 W

Services:
gas, food, lodging, RV, B&B

Located on the rim of the Great Basin, Paisley was the seasonal settlement of Northern Paiute and Klamath Native Americans. John C. Fremont, the first white explorer in the area, came in 1843. Immigrants from Paisley, Scotland settled the area in the 1870s. The post office opened in 1879 and the town incorporated in 1911. A pine lumber mill, now gone, was built here, and some gold was panned and mined

WOW Hall

near the town. A favorite story locals tell is about a man who found a large cache of gold near Deadhorse Lake, hid his find, but died before he could reclaim it. Legend says the stash has never been recovered. There are three century-old ranches in the area, including the ZX, whose headquarters are located in Paisley. The ranch is the largest in Oregon, covering an area 137 miles long and sixty-three miles wide. A 2002 fire scorched more than 34,000 acres in and around the Paisley community. The river that flows through town is the Chewaucan, which is Paiute for *'little potato.'* *'Chewa,'* an edible tuber with arrowhead-looking leaves, was a Native American staple. An annual Mosquito Festival, held every July, is the small town's main attraction.

Points of Interest

- **WOW Hall**
  (John and Highway 31)
  The Woodmen of the World (a life insurance society) building is in major disrepair. It stands next to a vacant lot where the Chewaucan Hotel existed. The hotel burned in the late 1970s. The WOW Hall was also the former home to Boy Scout Troop 14.

- **Paisley Ranger Station**
  (303 Highway 31)
  Built in the 1930s.

Paisley High School

- **Paisley Catholic Church** (*136 Green*)
  The church opened in 1895, was moved to its current location, and is now a private residence.

- **Old House** (*140 Green*)
  More than 100-years-old.

- **Paisley High School** (*260 Green*)
  Built in 1910 with beautiful columns that flank the entrance. An 1895 bell hangs in the tower.

- **Old House** (*280 Green*)
  First occupied in 1903.

- **Paisley United Methodist Church** (*504 Mill*)
  Opened in 1901.

- **Pioneer Saloon** (*327 Main*)
  Opened in 1883. The ornately carved bar, shipped around the horn, arrived in Paisley in 1905.

- **Old Paisley Store** (*437 Main*)
  Constructed in the early 1900s.

- **Paisley Cemetery** (*the end of W. Blue*)
  1881. It is also known as the Paisley IOOF Cemetery.

- **Virgil Conn House** (*314 Highway 31*)
  Dates to 1900.

- **Old Paisley School**
  The 1895 building is now The Old Church Inn Bed and Breakfast, named because the building formerly doubled as both the school and church. The inn is open June through September.

Pioneer Saloon

Virgil Conn House

Paisley to Summer Lake

Distance:
28.8 miles

Directions:
From the intersection of Highway 31 and John Street near the Chewaucan River, drive north on Highway 31.

Points En Route

(mileage from the bridge)

1.1 miles:
Shooting range.

1.4 miles:
Paisley Airport.

5.2 miles:
The outer rim of Summer Lake is visible. The lake dries in the summer and fills in the late spring.

5.9 miles:
Summer Lake Hot Springs. RV, camping, cabins. Natural hot springs are channeled into a series of outdoor pools before flowing into a covered swimming area. In 1843, John C. Fremont was the first explorer to bathe in the warm waters. The current bathhouse was constructed in 1925 and surrounds a pool of 106- to 113-degree water. The therapeutic waters contain boron, borate, calcium, chloride, flouride, magnesium, potassium, silica, sodium, and sulfate.

10.0 miles:
Rock outcropping to the left.

10.7 miles:
An old ranch flanks the road.

15.6 miles:
Grand, old farmhouse that is getting a facelift. Adjacent outbuildings are near collapse.

19.3 miles:
Evidence of the 2002 fire exists along the hillside.

23.1 miles:
Summer Lake/Harris Family Cemetery. Dates to 1885.

24.1 miles:
Harris House (51624 Highway 31): 1880s.

24.3 miles:
1890 Harris School. The school, built by the Harris family, closed in 1919, reopened in 1926, and closed for good in 1929.

26.0 miles:
Chimney remains of a farmhouse.

26.8 miles:
Old ranch house.

27.7 miles:
Summer Lake Wildlife Viewing Area and Oregon Department of Fish and Wildlife Building.

27.7 miles:
Interpretive kiosk and Lodge at Summer Lake (food and lodging).

28.8 miles:
Summer Lake

Harris School

Summer Lake

Elevation: 4348 feet

Location:
42.58.398 N • 120.46.625 W

Services:
gas, food, lodging, rest area

The small community was named after the lake located about five miles south, which was identified by John C. Fremont in 1843. The large, shallow, alkali lake extends almost twenty miles in the wet season. It is difficult to envision Summer Lake as it existed ten- to thirteen-thousand years ago, when it covered 461 square miles and exceeded 300 feet in depth. Big Horn Sheep were reintroduced to the area in 1991 and are frequently seen on the rocky outcroppings that parallel the highway. Nearby petroglyphs show evidence of the sheep that once lived here in abundance but disappeared when increasing numbers of settlers arrived in the early 1900s.

Points of Interest

- **Summer Lake Store**
  This building, constructed in the 1960s, replaced the original store.

- **Summer Lake Irrigation Association Building**
  The small building to the left of the store was the meeting place for the Irrigation Association. Circa 1920.

- **Summer Lake Rest Area**
  Across from the store are restrooms, an information kiosk, and a memorial to John C. Fremont.

Summer Lake Store

Basalt outcroppings above Summer Lake

Summer Lake to Silver Lake

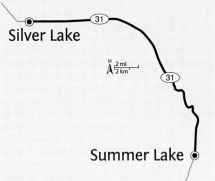

Distance:
  21.1 miles

Directions:
  From the rest area and general store, drive north on Highway 31 toward Silver Lake.

Points En Route

(mileage from the rest area)

2.2 miles:
  Camping, RV Park. Ana Reservoir.

2.8 miles:
  Snow zone and pullout.

4.6 miles:
  Fremont Viewpoint access road. Continue straight ahead on Highway 31.

5.9 miles:
  Summit of Picture Rock Pass, 4830 feet. From here the road narrows with a sharp drop-off to the left for 1.8 miles. The pass was named for the local petroglyphs.

9.1 miles:
  View of Table Rock.

11.8 miles:
  Old Lake Road (leads to Christmas Valley). Continue driving straight ahead on Highway 31.

13.6 miles:
  Table Rock to the right. Silver Lake, to the left, is a seasonal lake that often dries-up during the summer months.

18.1 miles:
  Crossing Mudrock Creek.

19.4 miles:
  Large ranch.

20.9 miles:
  Silver Lake Cemetery, dates to 1881. A large memorial and mass grave exist here for the forty-three people that lost their lives during the 1894 community Christmas dance party.

21.1 miles:
  Silver Lake

Table Rock

Silver Lake

Elevation: 4800 feet

Location:
43.07.680 N • 121.02.982 W

Services:
gas, food, lodging, RV

Silver Lake Church of the Bible

John C. Fremont is thought to be the first white visitor to the area, arriving in 1843. Named for the seasonal lake that is about six miles east, the Silver Lake Post Office opened in 1875, closed in 1880, and reopened in 1882. In 1894 the community suffered a terrible fate when a fire, at a Christmas Eve celebration on the second floor of Clayton Hall, killed forty-three citizens. The nearest doctor, 100 miles away in Lakeview, made a difficult, twenty-four hour buggy ride in the wind and snow to reach the injured and the dead. Dr. Bernard Daly cared for the victims three days and two nights without a break. The doors to the barn-like structure opened inward, so when the fire broke out, people panicked and unintentionally blocked the doors. Daly went on to help pass legislation that all public building exterior doors must open outwardly. Because Silver Lake no longer has its own school, students are bussed to the 1991 North Lake School where more than 250 students attend classes. Petrified wood is frequently found in the area.

Points of Interest

- **Silver Lake Market**
  (65555 Highway 31)
  The market is not that old.

- **Silver Lake Church of the Bible** *(65446 Highway 31)*
  Early 1900s.

- **Church Parsonage**
  (next to the church)
  Today it is Nana's Books.

- **Old House**
  (two doors south of the parsonage)
  Built in 1901.

Abandoned house

Silver Lake

Points of Interest (continued)

- **Silver Pole** (*across from the store*)
  The marker stands at the site of the tragic 1894 fire.

- **Former Silver Lake Mercantile and Grocery** (*65458 Highway 31*)
  Today the Desert Rose Quilt shop. The building was constructed in the early 1900s.

- **Old House** (*Center and 6th*)
  Thought to be the oldest in town.

- **Old Silver Lake School** (*Center and 3rd*)
  Dates to 1901.

- **Corum Park** (*Center*)
  The 1890-1916 log cabin home of George Lempke sits in the corner of the park. Amenities include picnic tables, playground, barbecue area, and pit toilets.

- **Cowboy Tree Restaurant** (*south on east road and follow signs*)
  Reservations a must. No credit cards.

Pioneer cabin at Corum Park

Silver Lake School

Silver Lake to Fort Rock

Distance:
24.0 miles

Directions:
From the intersection of Highway 31 and First Street at the Silver Lake Market, drive west on Highway 31 toward La Pine.

Points En Route

(mileage from the Silver Lake Market)

0.4 miles:
Silver Lake Ranger Station.

0.6 miles:
Crossing Silver Creek.

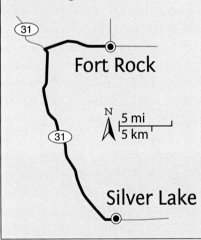

3.2 miles:
Old farmhouse with weathered outbuildings.

6.0 miles:
Basalt rim to the left.

8.0 miles:
Wildlife viewing area.

10.2 miles:
Basalt rim to the right. Note the different heights of the rim.

17.5 miles:
Fort Rock becomes visible in the distance.

17.9 miles:
Turn right onto Fort Rock Road. An information kiosk at the intersection describes the geology of the area. The highway is part of the Oregon Outback Scenic Byway.

20.1 miles:
Fort Rock looms larger in the distance.

24.0 miles:
Fort Rock

Fort Rock

Fort Rock

Elevation: 4332 feet

Location:
43.21.353 N • 121.03.479 W

Services:
gas, food

Water covered the Fort Rock area 50,000 to 100,000 years ago. Volcanic activity took place beneath the lakebed, forming a basalt and magma mountain. Water eventually eroded the mountainsides that today stand about 200 feet above the dry land surrounding it. William Sullivan, who settled here in 1873, named the formation for its fort-like shape. In 1936, 9,000- to 10,000-year-old sandals made of sagebrush were found in a cave just north of Fort Rock. While not open to the general public, that area is open to visitors who prearrange tours with the state of Oregon. The Fort Rock Post Office opened in 1908. The community of Fort Rock flourished prior to WWI and exists today much as it has for the past forty years. At one time, Fort Rock had a dentist, school, livery stable, saloon and card room, post office, dance and community hall, and two general stores. In 1964, cascades of ice oozed out of the volcanic fortress when the porous rock became saturated with water prior to a winter freeze. It is the only time in modern history that this is known to have happened.

Points of Interest

- **Homestead Open Air Museum**
  Many of the buildings were brought here from other sites in Lake County. The structures were collected and assembled in 1988. Buildings include the Sunset School, Fort Rock Mercantile, 1918 St. Rose of Lima Catholic Church, 1910 Menkenmaier

Fort Rock

Cabin, Widmer's Cabin (the land office), 1911 Belletable homestead, log cabin, water tower, Dr. Thom's 1905 medical office, an outhouse, and the 1912 Stratton House.

- **Fort Rock Natural and Interpretive Area**
  Primitive restrooms, parking lot, and hiking trails. The area allows visitors to explore the basalt walls of the fort.

- **Fort Rock Grange #758**
  Dedicated on June 16, 1930. The grange hosts an annual homesteaders reunion every second Sunday in September.

- **Fort Rock General Store**
  The old store is part of the open-air museum. The adjacent operating store was constructed in the 1960s.

- **Fort Rock Cemetery (1.5 miles from the store)**
  A small, family burial ground near the Natural Area. Dates to 1910.

- **Fort Rock State Park (1.6 miles from the store)**
  A tuff ring volcano that erupted about 100,000 years ago. A lake, once 183 feet deep, surrounded the volcano.

Sunset School at Homestead Open Air Museum

Fort Rock Grange

Side Trip – Hole in the Ground

Distance:

17.9 miles

Directions:

From the general store, drive west on Fort Rock Highway toward Highway 31.

Points En Route

(mileage from the general store)

0.0 miles:

Backtrack toward Highway 31.

6.3 miles:

Intersection of Fort Rock Highway and Highway 31. Turn right onto Highway 31.

6.6 miles:

A historical marker interprets Fort Rock geology here. The extinct volcano is a remnant of a maar volcano or tuff ring, formed when rising basalt magma encountered water and exploded violently. The debris, or tuff, fell back to earth around the volcanic vent to form a steep-walled fort-like ring. Over time the basin filled with a shallow lake which breached the south rim of the tuff ring, cutting a terrace about sixty-feet above the floor of the valley.

6.6 miles:

Horse Ranch RV Park.

8.6 miles:

Entering Deschutes County.

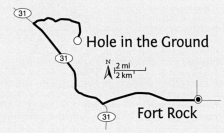

13.4 miles:

Turn right onto Breakup Road near state highway milepost marker 22. Gravel road for 4.5 miles.

16.3 miles:

Gravel becomes dirt. Not recommended for low clearance vehicles. Go slowly.

16.5 miles:

At the 'Y' go right.

17.7 miles:

Turn left at the 'Y.'

17.9 miles:

Hole in the Ground. A circular, one-mile in diameter crater formed when the volcano erupted about 15,000 years ago. Boulders as large as eight feet in diameter blew skyward, landing more than two miles from the crater.

Hole in the Ground

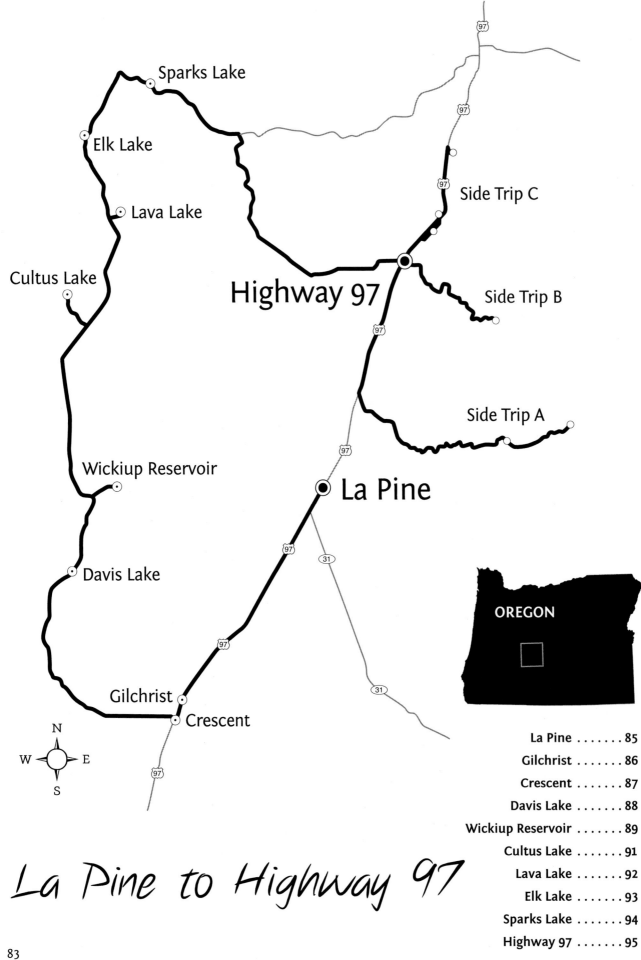

Sparks Lake

Elk Lake

Lava Lake

Side Trip C

Cultus Lake

Highway 97

Side Trip B

Side Trip A

Wickiup Reservoir

La Pine

Davis Lake

OREGON

Gilchrist

Crescent

N
W E
S

La Pine to Highway 97

Through the Land of Lakes to Obsidian, Lava Cast Forest and Caves

La Pine to Highway 97 (100 miles)

This tour circles an area of high lakes and the most prolific volcanic region in Oregon. Beginning in the relatively new community of La Pine, the route continues toward Gilchrist, one of a handful of 'company' towns - this one formerly owned and controlled by the Gilchrist Lumber Company. The town where nearly every house has a metal roof was once called 'Brown Town' because every home was painted the same brown color. Old buildings appear much as they did in the 1930s when lumber was king.

From Gilchrist, travel on Century Drive and Cascade Lakes Highway to explore scenic volcanic activity areas, and visit the many lakes in the higher elevations of Central Oregon that are home to some of the best fishing our state has to offer.

At the end of the route, three separate and distinct side trips are outlined: A) Newberry Crater (Paulina and East Lakes); B) Lava Cast Forest; and C) Lava River Caves, Lava Lands Visitor Center, Lava Butte, and the High Desert Museum. None will disappoint!

Lava Lands fire lookout

La Pine

Elevation: 4236 feet

Location:
43.40.465 N • 121.30.316 W

Services:
gas, food, lodging, RV

Fur trappers, who ventured over the Cascade Mountains in search of beaver, arrived in the La Pine area in the 1840s. Although it was formed in the late 1800s, La Pine didn't incorporate until 2006, making it one of Oregon's newest cities. Alfred A. Aya named La Pine for the abundance of pine trees that grew here. Lapine, the name of the post office when it opened in 1910, was changed to La Pine in 1951. 1920s 'Lapine' had a livery stable, blacksmith, bank, hotel, dairy, mercantile, meat market, and its own newspaper. Growth slowed for a time due to lack of water and sewer, but the town today is one of the fastest growing in Oregon. La Pine calls itself the 'Gateway to Recreation.'

Little Deschutes Grange Hall

South Ice Cave

Points of Interest

- **Little Deschutes Grange Hall #939** (*51518 Morson*)
Built in 1912 and one of the oldest buildings in La Pine.

- **La Pine Community Park**
(*0.5 miles on Finley Butte Road*)
Picnic area, community hall, sports fields, and restrooms.

- **Finley Butte**
(*3.0 miles on Finley Butte Road*)

- **South Ice Cave**
(*25.0 miles on Finley Butte Road*)
Travel twenty-five miles on Finley Butte Road/Forest Road 22 to the ice cave. The road is paved and offers interesting scenery en route. However, due to the cave's 4800 foot elevation, it is important to check road conditions before heading out. The cave is known for its ice sculptures, especially during spring.

La Pine to Gilchrist

Distance:
15.8 miles

Directions:
From the intersection of Highway 97 and Finley Butte Road, drive south on Highway 97.

Points En Route

(mileage from the intersection of Highway 97 and Finley Butte Road)

4.0 miles:
Entering Klamath County.

8.4 miles:
Jack Pine Village, an RV park.

13.6 miles:
Entering Gilchrist National Forest.

15.8 miles:
Gilchrist

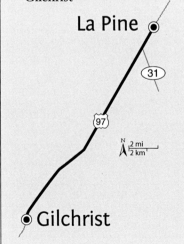

Gilchrist

Elevation: 4845 feet

Location:
43.28.591 N • 121.41.188 W

Services:
gas, food

The Gilchrist Lumber Company formed the town in 1938 and the post office opened the same year. The original post office boxes are still used today. As a 'company' town, all of the houses and stores belonged to the company owned and operated by Frank and Mary Gilchrist who came here from Mississippi. At one time the company owned or controlled more than 100,000 acres of timber and land. Gilchrist was the last company town in Oregon when it fired all workers and closed in 1991. The one hundred company homes and businesses were then sold to individuals. Prior to the company closure, every home was painted brown, giving Gilchrist the nickname 'Brown Town.' Although painted different colors today, nearly every house in Gilchrist has a metal roof.

Gilchrist Mill

Points of Interest

- **Gilchrist Mall** (*Highway 97*)
  This mall comprised the 'town' where company owned businesses were connected. A bowling alley, pool hall, movie theater, clothing store, grocery, bank, hardware store, mercantile, restaurant, library, and a radio station were all located in this complex.

- **Gilchrist Movie Theater** (*138465 Michigan*)
  Built across the street from the Mall in the 1940s.

- **Gilchrist Community Church** (*Manzanita*)
  Dates to 1939.

- **Gilchrist School** (*Mountain View*)
  Built by the WPA in 1939.

- **Gilchrist Mill** (*across Highway 97 on Sawmill Road*)
  The mill, partially in use, opened in 1938. The Little Deschutes River was dammed and used as the log pond. A fish ladder is visible where the river was blocked.

Gilchrist to Crescent

Distance:
0.3 miles

Directions:
From the intersection of Highway 97 and Mt. View at the Gilchrist Mall, travel south on Highway 97.

Points En Route

(mileage from the intersection of Highway 97 and Mt. View)

0.3 miles:
Crescent

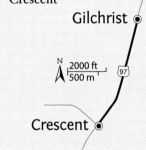

Crescent

Elevation: 4837 feet

Location:
43.27.820 N • 121.41.708 W

Services:
gas, food, lodging, RV

Crescent was an important trading post on The Dalles-California Highway (Highway 97). Some Gilchrist Mill workers also lived here. Crescent was known as a rough and tumble community, complete with bars and brothels. The current population is less than 800 residents, many who live here seasonally.

Crescent Boarding House

Points of Interest

- **Mohawk Restaurant and Lounge** *(136726 Highway 97)*
  The upstairs served as a brothel during timber heydays.

- **Crescent Boarding House** *(136617 Highway 97)*
  The old boarding house, located within walking distance to the mill, housed many mill and timber workers. It was conveniently located across the street from the 'restaurant and lounge.'

Mohawk Restaurant

Crescent to Davis Lake

Distance:
  15.9 miles

Directions:
  From the intersection of Highway 97 and Crescent Cut-off Road at the Shell Gas Station, drive west on Crescent Cut-off Road.

Points En Route

(mileage from the Shell Gas Station)

0.1 miles:
  The 1956 Crescent Community Club building.

4.1 miles:
  Odell Butte.

6.1 miles:
  Basalt flows.

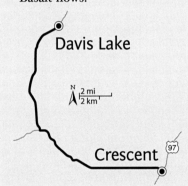

6.6 miles:
  Crescent Creek Campground.

6.7 miles:
  Entering Deschutes National Forest.

8.8 miles:
  Turn right onto Cascade Lakes Highway, also referred to as the Cascade Lakes Scenic Byway.

11.1 miles:
  Scenic Byway Wayside. Interpretive plaques.

12.1 miles:
  West Davis Lake Boat Launch access road (five miles). Maiden Lake Trail access is six miles.

14.7 miles:
  Pullout, interpretive signs, and views of Davis Lake.

15.1 miles:
  Turn left toward East Davis Lake Campground. A gravel road winds through a fire-damaged area.

15.9 miles:
  Davis Lake and East Davis Lake Campground

Davis Lake

Elevation: 3694 feet

Location:
43.35.301 N • 121.51.241 W

Services:
camping, pit toilets, tables

Davis Lake is a shallow (a mean depth of nine feet and maximum depth of twenty-two feet) lake that covers a little over six square miles. Davis Lake was formed when a lava flow blocked Odell Creek. The lake is fed by Odell Creek and Ranger Creek and ebbs and flows in size depending upon the season. Bass were illegally introduced into the lake in the 1990s and are more abundant than trout. Davis Lake is a fly-fishing only lake with three campground areas. Water is available in two of the three campgrounds.

East Davis Lake Campground

Davis Lake to Wickiup Reservoir

Distance:
7.8 miles

Directions:
Return to the Cascade Lakes Highway and travel north.

Points En Route

(mileage from East Davis Road and Cascade Lakes Highway)

1.3 miles:
Davis Lake access road (leads to an undeveloped area).

2.8 miles:
Entering Deschutes County.

3.8 miles:
Lava Flow Campground.

4.5 miles:
The road parallels lava flows.

6.1 miles:
Turn right toward Wickiup Reservoir Campground. Travel on 1.7 miles of gravel road.

7.8 miles:
Reservoir Campground. Restrooms, picnic area, campsites, boat launch area.

7.8 miles:
Wickiup Reservoir

Wickiup Reservoir

Elevation: 4469 feet

Location:
43.39.869 N • 121.47.853 W

Services:
camping

Wickiup is the second largest reservoir in the state of Oregon. Built in 1949 when the Deschutes River was dammed, it is the largest body of water in the Cascades. The deepest spot in the reservoir is seventy feet, with an average depth of about twenty feet. The lake is more than 10,000 acres in size. Wickiup is noted for its German Brown fishing – reputedly the best in the state. There are six campgrounds, each with a boat launch. Travelers are cautioned not to drink the lake water, even if boiled.

Lava flow

Wickiup Reservoir

Wickiup Reservoir to Cultus Lake

Distance:
13.8 miles

Directions:
Return to Cascade Lakes Highway. From the intersection of Reservoir Campground access road and Cascade Lakes Highway, travel north toward Cultus Lake.

Points En Route

(mileage from the intersection of Cascade Lakes Highway and Reservoir Access Road)

1.5 miles:
Lake Campground.

5.4 miles:
Cascade Lakes Highway intersects with South Century Drive. South Century Drive leads to Twin Lakes and Crane Prairie. This route continues straight ahead on Cascade Lakes Highway. Crane Prairie is a reservoir, formed in 1922 when the Deschutes River, Cultus Creek, Cold Creek, Quinn River, Deer Creek, and Cultus River were dammed at the confluence of these bodies of water. The reservoir was named for the abundance of cranes that feed in the river and lake and was formed to control water levels and flooding. Crane Prairie is more than 4940 acres with twenty-four miles of shoreline, only ten to twenty feet in depth, and is known for its large rainbow trout. The record fish weighed more than nineteen pounds. Locals say four- to ten-pound catches are common, but only one trout over sixteen inches in length may be kept. There are several different campgrounds around the reservoir with varied facilities. Free campgrounds have limited facilities. Broken Top, the Three Sisters, and Mt. Bachelor are easily seen from the reservoir.

7.0 miles:
Pullout for wildlife viewing.

8.0 miles:
Rock Creek Campground access.

9.1 miles:
Osprey Point Interpretive Trail.

9.5 miles:
Quinn River Campground.

11.8 miles:
Turn left toward Cultus Lake Campground and Resort.

12.5 miles:
Stay straight. Left is Little Cultus Lake (three miles). Irish and Taylor Lakes are seven miles. To the right is Cultus Corral Horse Camp (two miles).

13.5 miles:
Cultus Lake Resort and Restaurant. The resort has twenty-three cabins, a marina, and sells groceries.

13.8 miles:
Cultus Lake Campground and lake access

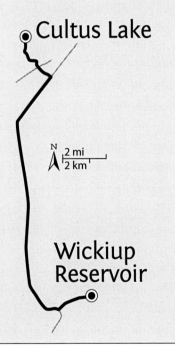

Cultus Lake

N 2 mi / 2 km

Wickiup Reservoir

Cultus Lake

Elevation: 4690 feet

Location:
43.49.770 N • 121.49.939 W

Services:
gas, food, lodging, camping

Cultus Lake is glacially carved and covers 790 acres. The two-mile-long lake located near the base of Irish Mountain and Cultus Mountain is more than 200 feet at its greatest depth. In addition to the resort, three separate campgrounds are located on the lake. Rainbow trout and Mackinaw are said to be plentiful in this deep lake and motorboats are allowed, making it popular for anglers. A 17.5-pound lake trout (Mackinaw) was taken from this body of water in 1996.

Cultus Lake to Lava Lake

Distance:
8.4 miles

Directions:
Return to the intersection of Cultus Lake Campground access road (4635) and Cascade Lakes Highway. Turn left onto Cascade Lakes Highway, traveling north.

Points En Route

(mileage from the intersection of Cultus Lake Campground access road and the Cascade Lakes Highway)

1.2 miles:
Junction of Highway 97 (Cow Meadow Trail Access Road) and Cascade Lakes Highway. Stay on Cascade Lakes Highway.

2.1 miles:
The road parallels the Deschutes River and affords many pullouts and river access.

4.7 miles:
Trailhead to the left and Deschutes Bridge to the right.

5.5 miles:
Mile Camp day-use area.

6.2 miles:
View of Mt. Bachelor.

7.0 miles:
Trailhead.

7.5 miles:
Turn right toward Lava Lake Resort.

8.1 miles:
Turn right onto Lava Lake and Little Lava Lake access road.

8.4 miles:
Lava Lake (campground, lodge, store)

Cultus Lake

Lava Lake

Elevation: 4790 feet

Location:

43.54.881 N • 121.45.088 W

Services:

gas, food, lodging, camping, RV

Lava Lake and Little Lava Lake comprise the Lava Lakes recreation area. Underground springs, located in the northeast corner of Lava Lake, fill the larger body of water. When it overflows, water empties into Little Lava Lake. There are no surface streams that feed into either of these lakes. Bull Trout, Redband Trout, and White Fish flourish in the cool waters of the lakes. Lava Lake is at 4790 feet elevation, compared to Little Lava Lake, which is at 4750 feet. Lava Lake covers 350 acres, averages only twenty-five feet in depth, and has forty-three RV/camp sites, showers, restrooms, boat launch, and picnicking. Little Lava Lake is 130 acres and produced a nine-pound, six-ounce brook trout, the state record. Little Lava Lake has restrooms, camping, showers, boat launch, swimming, and picnicking. Both lakes are open from May through October.

Lava Lake and Mt. Bachelor

Lava Lake to Elk Lake

Distance:
5.3 miles

Directions:
Return to the intersection of Cascade Lakes Highway and Lava Lakes Campground access road. Continue north (turn right) onto Cascade Lakes Highway.

Points En Route

(mileage from the intersection of Cascade Lakes Highway and Lava Lakes Campground access road)

2.7 miles:
Forest Road 4625 is Elk Lake Loop, which is the access to Hosmer Lake and the east side of Elk Lake. Continue straight ahead on Cascade Lakes Highway.

3.3 miles:
Trailhead.

3.8 miles:
Beach day-use area.

4.3 miles:
Elk Lake pullout and viewpoint. Information kiosk.

5.2 miles:
Elk Lake campground and day use area.

5.3 miles:
Elk Lake

Elk Lake

Elevation: 4884 feet

Location:
43.58.944 N • 121.48.447 W

Services:
gas, food, lodging, camping, boat launch

The lake was formed when lava restricted the flow of several mountain streams. Because of heavy, year-round recreational use here, Bend has a branch post office at Elk Lake. USFS Ranger Roy Harvey named the lake for the large herd of elk that roamed the area and swam in its waters. Large numbers of seven- to ten-inch Kokanee Trout found in the clear lake waters make it a popular fishing spot for anglers. In addition, thousands of Brook Trout are planted every year, ranging from ten to eighteen inches. Elk Lake is a natural lake that covers about 400 acres and averages twenty-five to seventy-five feet in depth. Many burnt trees are evidence of the 1998 forest fire. The lake freezes over most winters.

Elk Lake

Elk Lake to Sparks Lake

Distance:
8.4 miles

Directions:
From the intersection of Elk Lake Resort access road and Cascade Lakes Highway, continue north on Cascades Lakes Highway.

Points En Route

(mileage from the intersection of Elk Lake Resort access road and Cascade Lakes Highway)

0.3 miles:
Junction with Elk Lake Loop. Continue straight.

1.7 miles:
Quinn Meadow Horse Camp access road.

2.8 miles:
Mirror Lakes Trailhead.

3.3 miles:
Lava flows.

4.1 miles:
Devil's Lake Trailhead.

4.5 miles:
Pullout with interpretive signs and Devil's Lake views. The Cascade Lakes Highway heads due east at this point.

5.6 miles:
Interpretive sign.

6.2 miles:
Green Lakes Trailhead.

6.7 miles:
Turn right toward Sparks Lake Recreation Area.

6.8 miles:
Turn left to Sparks Lake access and boat ramp. The road is rough for the next 1.6 miles. Note: a right turn at 6.8 miles leads to Soda Creek Campground.

8.4 miles:
Sparks Lake

Sparks Lake

Elevation: 5460 feet

Location:
44.01.467 N • 121.43.879 W

Services:
camping, pit toilets, boat ramp

Sparks Lake was named after pioneer stockman Lige Sparks. Explorers Dr. John S. Newberry and Lts. Phil Sheridan and R.L. Williamson first visited the lake in 1855. Volcanic activity that occurred more than 10,000 years ago blocked the Deschutes River to form the lake. The lake covers about 400 acres and has a maximum depth of twelve feet. A boat-launch area, and picnic and camping facilities are available. The lake is fly-fishing only. Seven mountains can be seen from Sparks Lake, including Mt. Bachelor, the Three Sisters, Broken Top, Mt. Jefferson, and Tumalo Mountain.

Sparks Lake

Sparks Lake to Highway 97

Distance:
24.4 miles

Directions:
Return to the intersection of Sparks Lake access road and North Cascade Lakes Highway. From this intersection, continue east on North Cascade Lakes Highway.

Points En Route

(mileage from the intersection of Sparks Lake access road and North Cascade Lakes Highway)

2.1 miles:
Todd Lake. Day-use area.

3.5 miles:
Mt. Bachelor to the right. Elevation: 9065 feet.

3.8 miles:
Mt. Bachelor West Village Lodge.

4.1 miles:
Dutchman Flat Sno-Park.

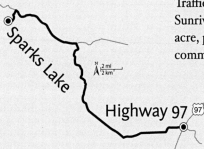

4.4 miles:
Mt. Bachelor Sunrise Lodge.

6.7 miles:
Highway divides.

7.0 miles:
Turn right, heading south on Forest Road 45 toward Sunriver and La Pine.

11.1 miles:
Edison Butte Sno-Park.

18.4 miles:
Keep left, heading east toward Sunriver.

20.3 miles:
Leaving Deschutes National Forest.

21.8 miles:
Crossing Deschutes River.

22.4 miles:
Spring River Road becomes South Century Drive.

22.7 miles:
Traffic signal and access to Sunriver. Sunriver is a 3300-acre, privately planned resort community, located on the Deschutes River and bordered by the Cascade Mountains. Sunriver is located on the grounds of WWII Camp Abbott, a facility designed to train troops for combat. The training center was named after Brigadier-General Larcom Abbott, who camped near here in 1855. The camp opened in 1942, was short-lived, and closed in 1944. While most of the old camp was razed, the officer's club remains, and what is known as the 'Great Hall,' is under Sunriver Resort management. The name Sunriver was given to the community by developers John Gray and Donald McCallum. A park, nature center, observatory, marina, airport, business park, school, shopping village, swimming pools, riding stables, restaurants, three golf courses, and many tennis courts help make Sunriver a desirable destination. 1700 people live here year-round and thousands more own recreational property. The post office opened in 1969, the same year the young community was established.

23.0 miles:
Roundabout. Keep right on South Century Drive toward Highway 97.

24.4 miles:
Highway 97

Side Trip A – Paulina Lake and East Lake

Distance:
26.0 miles

Directions:
At the intersection of South Century Drive and Highway 97, go south on Highway 97.

Points En Route

(mileage from the Highway 97 south-bound on-ramp)

6.0 miles:
Leaving Deschutes National Forest.

7.4 miles:
La Pine State Park.

8.6 miles:
Turn left onto Paulina-East Lake Road, traveling toward Newberry Caldera, Paulina Lake, and East Lake.

10.3 miles:
Entering Deschutes National Forest.

11.4 miles:
Ogden Group Camp.

11.6 miles:
Prairie Campground.

11.8 miles:
McKay Crossing Campground.

14.0 miles:
Six-mile Sno-Park.

18.1 miles:
Ten-mile Sno-Park.

19.8 miles:
Newberry National Monument Entrance Station. This is a fee area.

20.8 miles:
Paulina Falls.

21.0 miles:
Newberry Wildlife Refuge.

21.1 miles:
Paulina Lodge, 1929. Services include gas, food, lodging, and boat docks.

21.1 miles:
Paulina Lake. Paulina Lake and East Lake were both formed inside the more than 500 square-mile Newberry Crater. Named after Chief Paulina, Paulina Lake is one of the deepest in the state and is over 250 feet deep and covers 1531 acres. Snow, rain, and hot springs feed the lake, giving it a brilliant blue color. Newberry Volcano first erupted about 400,000 years ago, and the caldera formed about 80,000 years ago. Deposits of lava and pumice divided the body of water in the crater in half about 6000 years ago, forming the two lakes. Geothermal activity in the area includes hot springs located at the northeast side of Paulina Lake and the southeast side of East Lake. Ten campgrounds, seven day-use areas, and eleven trails and trailheads exist in the Newberry Caldera area. The large volcano has a twenty-mile diameter and a volume of more than eighty million cubic miles!

21.2 miles:
Paulina Lake Visitors Center.

Points En Route continues on next page.

Paulina Lake

Side Trip A (continued)

22.4 miles:
Paulina Peak (to the right) and Paulina Campground (to the left). Paulina Peak, at 7989 feet in height, is the remaining portion of the once immense Newberry Volcano.

22.4 miles:
Chief Paulina Horse Camp (right), and Newberry Group Camp (left).

22.9 miles:
Little Crater Campground.

23.3 miles:
Big Obsidian Flow. This 170 million cubic yard flow was formed when Newberry Volcano erupted about 1300 years ago. It is one of the youngest geologic events in Oregon. There is an easy half-mile interpretive hike through the flow, but visitors are reminded that removing obsidian is prohibited.

25.0 miles:
East Lake Campground.

25.7 miles:
East Lake Hot Springs and Boat Ramp.

26.0 miles:
East Lake. Located east of Paulina Lake, East Lake is the smaller of the two and is less than 1050 acres. Slightly higher in elevation than Paulina Lake, East Lake has a depth of 180 feet at its deepest point and averages around fifty feet. Snow, rain, and a hot spring fill this lake and the warm temperatures accelerate the growth of Kokanee, Brown Trout, and Rainbow Trout. Lake amenities include two main campgrounds with 200 camping sites, cabins, boat launch, playground, RV parking, a resort, and a general store that was built in 1915. Hot springs are located in the southeast corner of the park. A twenty-two pound German Brown Trout was caught in East Lake. In October 2012, the Fly Fishing National Championships were held here.

Big Obsidian Flow

East Lake Resort

East Lake

Side Trip B – Lava Cast Forest

Distance:
  9.0 miles

Directions:
  From the intersection of South Century Drive, Highway 97, and Forest Road 9720, take Forest Road 9720 east toward Lava Cast Forest.

Points En Route

(mileage from the intersection of South Century Drive, Highway 97, and Forest Road 9720)

0.1 miles:
  Striping on pavement ends.

0.6 miles:
  Camp Abbott, Lava Butte. Pavement ends. The road is rough for the next 8.4 miles.

8.0 miles:
  Entering Newberry National Volcanic Monument.

8.1 miles:
  Hoffman Island Trail, a one-mile hike.

8.3 miles:
  Keep right on Forest Road 950. The road narrows with lava beds on the left.

8.8 miles:
  Fee area reminder sign.

9.0 miles:
  Lava Cast Forest. Approximately 7000 years ago, Newberry Crater released about five miles of lava into a pine forest. As the lava flowed, it surrounded and burned the trees, but a cast impression of the pines remained. Hundreds of casts can be viewed on the mile-long, paved, self-guided walk through the lava flow. A small fee is required and the hike is rated as easy. The day-use area was established by the Forest Service in 1942 and is open only in summer. Here you'll find a parking lot, a few picnic tables, and pit toilets.

Lava Cast Forest Trail

Tree casts

Lava flow

Side Trip C – Lava River Cave, Lava Lands Visitors Center and Lava Butte, and High Desert Museum

Distance:

12.3 miles

Directions:

From the intersection of South Century Drive and Highway 97 exit 153, go north on Highway 97.

Points En Route

(mileage from the intersection of South Century Drive and Highway 97)

1.1 miles:

Turn right at Exit 151.

1.7 miles:

Stop sign. Turn right onto Cottonwoods Road, traveling toward Lava River Cave and Lava Lands Visitor Center (fee area).

2.6 miles:

Lava River Cave. The cave is an example of a lava tube, formed when Newberry Crater spewed lava about 80,000 years ago. At more that one mile in length, the cave is the longest lava tube in Oregon. A hunter, Leander Dillman, discovered the cave in 1889, even though Native Americans knew of and used the cave for thousands of years. There is a charge to enter the cave and a small charge to rent a lantern. Gas or kerosene lanterns are not allowed. Temperatures are cool, so bring a jacket or sweatshirt. Bats are quite common in the cave area, so take care not to come into contact with them. Bats use echolocation to hunt, navigate,

and communicate. They eat more than 1000 insects every hour, can live twenty years, and hibernate during the winter. Bats can fly twenty to thirty miles an hour and frequently will travel in excess of one hundred miles a night. Bats hang upside down because that is the best position for take-off. Baby bats are called pups.

3.7 miles:

Stop sign. Turn right toward Lava Lands Visitors Center.

3.8 miles:

Lava Lands Visitor Center (fee area). Visitors can obtain a thirty-minute pass to drive to the top of Lava Butte where parking, water, restrooms, hiking trails,

Lava River Cave

Lava Lands

and interpretive signs are available in addition to the fantastic, panoramic view. Lava Butte is a cinder cone that rises 500 feet above the lava flow at an elevation of 5020 feet and was formed about 7000 years ago during Newberry Volcanic activity. Lava Butte only erupted once, unlike many other volcanic mountains and buttes. The steep, spiraling road to the top of the butte was constructed in 1933, widened in 1946, and paved in 1950. In 1966, more than twenty astronauts trained for lunar missions in the lava fields around the butte. The Visitors Center is open seasonally.

3.9 miles:
Turn left toward Highway 97.

5.8 miles:
Turn right onto Highway 97, heading toward Bend.

8.4 miles:
Lava Butte Pass, elevation 4510 feet.

11.5 miles:
Leaving Deschutes National Forest.

12 miles:
Turn right toward High Desert Museum.

12.3 miles:
High Desert Museum. The museum opened in 1982 on 135 acres of ground and was the realization of a dream of Donald

M. Kerr, a biology student with a passion for natural history. Numerous interesting exhibits that frequently change make the museum a frequent destination for visitors of all ages. A gift shop and restrooms are available in the museum complex.

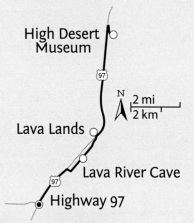

Lava Lands

Covered wagon at High Desert Museum

High Desert Museum

Notes

About the Author

Author Steve Arndt grew up in rural Independence, Oregon during the state's centennial, a setting that kindled his curiosity about the region's history.

His uncle, William Gilbaugh, now a retired Washington State park ranger and noted northwest photographer, further ignited his passion by occasionally taking Steve on tours of Oregon and Washington back roads and byways.

After earning a degree in elementary education from Oregon College of Education (now Western Oregon University), Steve completed advanced degree coursework in special education at OCE, school administration at Portland State University, and his school superintendent credentials at the University of Oregon. In his forty-year career in education, Steve served various Oregon public schools as teacher and administrator, and completed his last nineteen years in higher education as senior associate professor of teacher education, including ten years as a department chair.

Steve, his wife Diane, and their now-grown children have spent many weekends and school vacations exploring Oregon back roads and off-the-beaten places. Today, their car is filled with child safety seats for young granddaughters that have begun road trips with grandma and grandpa. Both Steve and Diane continue to fill important roles at the Woodburn United Methodist Church and enjoy volunteering in the Woodburn community and participating in various philanthropic groups and endeavors.

Amanda Arndt Vega

Although Diane, a retired music educator and professional singer, has no formal training in photography, she enjoys her role as photographer, organizer, and proofreader of Steve's book series.

Answers from page vi:

1 Sun Stones are the state gem;
   Thunder Eggs are the state rock.

2 Colliding Rivers. It is the only place where
   two rivers run head-on into each other.

3 Bly

4 Olene

5 Crack in the Ground

6 Captain Jack, Chief of the Modocs

7 Chiloquin

8 Bohemian Mine

9 Every house was painted brown.

10 Forty-three townspeople were killed in a fire.